The Media and the Public

Communication in the Public Interest

Communication has never been more important than in our current cultural moment. From the growing monopolization of global media, to human rights issues, health campaigns, and issues of free speech and society, communication has real political and ethical consequences. The books in this ICA Wiley-Blackwell *Communication in the Public Interest* series are accessible and definitive treatments of subjects central to understanding communication and its intersections to the wider world; they will widen understanding, encourage discussion, and illuminate the importance of communicating about issues that affect people's lives.

Already published

Susan Moeller: *Packaging Terrorism: Co-opting the News for Politics and Profit*
Roxanne Parrott: *Talking about Health: Why Communication Matters*
Stephen Coleman and Karen Ross: *The Media and the Public: "Them" and "Us" in Media Discourse*

Forthcoming

Nadia Caidi: *Right to Know: Information Post 9/11*
Michael Delli Carpini: *Beyond the Ivory Tower: Communication and the Public Interest*

The Media and the Public

"Them" and "Us" in Media Discourse

Stephen Coleman and Karen Ross

A John Wiley & Sons, Ltd., Publication

This edition first published 2010
© 2010 Stephen Coleman and Karen Ross

Blackwell Publishing was acquired by John Wiley & Sons in February 2007. Blackwell's
publishing program has been merged with Wiley's global Scientific, Technical, and
Medical business to form Wiley-Blackwell.

Registered Office
John Wiley & Sons Ltd, The Atrium, Southern Gate, Chichester, West Sussex, PO19 8SQ,
United Kingdom

Editorial Offices
350 Main Street, Malden, MA 02148–5020, USA
9600 Garsington Road, Oxford, OX4 2DQ, UK
The Atrium, Southern Gate, Chichester, West Sussex, PO19 8SQ, UK

For details of our global editorial offices, for customer services, and for information about
how to apply for permission to reuse the copyright material in this book please see our
website at www.wiley.com/wiley-blackwell.

The right of Stephen Coleman and Karen Ross to be identified as the authors of this work
has been asserted in accordance with the Copyright, Designs and Patents Act 1988.

Library of Congress Cataloging-in-Publication Data
Coleman, Stephen, 1957–
    The media and the public : "them" and "us" in media discourse / Stephen Coleman
and Karen Ross.
        p. cm. – (Communication in the public interest)
    Includes bibliographical references and index.
    ISBN 978-1-4051-6040-7 (hardcover : alk. paper) – ISBN 978-1-4051-6041-4
(pbk. : alk. paper)   1. Mass media–Audiences.   2. Mass media and culture.
3. Mass media and public opinion.   4. Mass media–Social aspects.   5. Public interest.
I. Ross, Karen, 1957–   II. Title.
    P96.A83R57 2010
    302.23–dc22

                                                                    2009046291

A catalogue record for this book is available from the British Library.

Set in 10.5/13pt Photina by Graphicraft Limited, Hong Kong
Printed and bound in Malaysia by Vivar Printing Sdn Bhd

01   2010

Contents

Acknowledgments

A few years ago (although it now seems a lifetime away), one of us was sitting with a group of colleagues invited by Elizabeth Swayze at Wiley-Blackwell, talking enthusiastically about ICA's new book series, *Communication in the Public Interest*. Out of that engaging discussion came the idea for this book and this is by way of saying that its gestation period was more elephant than human (and then some) because life just gets in the way. So we would like to thank Elizabeth for staying with us for the long haul, for keeping the faith with enviable patience and good humor; also to Margot, Jayne, and Annie for their various skills in keeping us on message until the very end. We are pleased to finally be writing these acknowledgments, a pleasure that at some points looked to be a rather unlikely prospect.

Stephen Coleman would like to thank his colleagues at the Institute of Communications Studies, University of Leeds, for providing the intellectual stimulation that has sustained this project — and also colleagues from the Oxford Internet Institute and the Reuters Institute for the Study of Journalism at the University of Oxford, who have always been interested in discussing new ideas. As ever, my work has benefited from the influence of good friends and research partners, such as Jay Blumler, John Corner, and David Morrison, for whose encouragement and patience I am always grateful. I am very happy to now be able to add Karen Ross to that list; her sense of fun and social engagement makes writing with her feel like a pleasure rather than a chore. As ever, my wife, Bernadette has given me the kind of support that should never be taken for granted.

Karen Ross would like to extend a personal thanks to Elizabeth Swayze for being the dream commissioning editor, always supportive and encouraging despite deadline failure and other authorial misdemeanors. I would also like to thank innumerable colleagues and students who, down the years, have provided intellectual challenges and brought personal joys, all of which bolster and sustain the crazy life of the academic in the noughties. Particular thanks must go to my transatlantic colleague, friend, and writing partner, Carolyn Byerly, whose friendship and collegiality has been and continues to be invaluable. My other good friends and colleagues, Dafna Lemish, Katharine Sarikakis, and Virginia Nightingale and my new-ish chums at Liverpool have all provided inspirations of different character. My sister Elizabeth and my daughters Josie and Lizzie, have kept me grounded and sane and this book, like my others, is a tribute to the strength of family and friendship. Lastly, I would like to thank my co-writer and conspirator, Stephen Coleman, who took up my invitation to co-write this book with enthusiasm and whose insight and intelligence has made it what it is.

Introduction

Them and Us: Meet Joe the Plumber

October 12, 2008. Shrewsbury Street in the white, working-class, Lincoln Green district of Holland, Ohio. The culminating stage of a dramatic and exhausting presidential election campaign. Two faces of representation exchange suspicious glances. On the left, Barack Obama, who is canvassing as Democratic nominee for the US presidency. In his successful

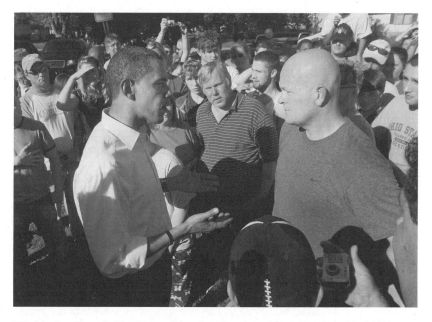

Figure 1 Barack Obama and Joe the Plumber, Ohio, October 12, 2008. Photo © Joe Raedle/Getty Images.

bid to represent the interests and aspirations of the American public, he is destined to redefine what an American president might look like; where he might come from; the sense in which he might use terms such as "we" and "us." On the right, within hand-shaking distance of the candidate, but conspicuously not looking inclined to shake hands, is the man who, after this media-recorded exchange, will answer to the name of Joe the Plumber. The latter asks Obama whether he "believes in the American Dream" and goes on to criticize his tax policies, which he claims would injure small businessmen like himself. He looks angry, skeptical, uncharmed by the seductive words of the visiting politician. The surrounding crowd may or may not sympathize with Joe, but they don't look happy. Their eyes signal leeriness and bemusement. Their stances embody suspicion. Two kinds of representation are at work here: the politician who claims to *speak for* the public and the "ordinary guy" who claims to *speak as* the public. Leadership versus mimesis; professionalism versus populism; "them" versus "us." This is more than a snapshot of a passing moment on the campaign trail; it is an image that captures the complexity and ambivalence of what it means to speak of, as, or for the public in the early twenty-first century.

Three days later, in the final televized presidential debate held at Hofstra University, Obama's Republican rival, John McCain, refers repeatedly to Joe the Plumber. In fact, he refers to him no fewer than 19 times during the one-hour debate – and Obama, not be left out, refers to him four times. Joe the Plumber had become an iconic symbol of democratic politics. Like Everyman, the Man in the Street, Vox Populi, John Q. Public, Joe Sixpack, and the Man on the Clapham Omnibus before him, it was Joe's job to personify an entity that is never fully witnessed but endlessly discussed, addressed, and depicted: The Public. Joe the Plumber's fame was as a symbolic representation of this discrete entity, the public. He is a symbolic embodiment of that which can never be truly embodied, because, by definition, the public is not an entity to be characterized but a space to be filled in. In short, both Obama and Joe the Plumber were competing to speak on behalf of the public. The political theorist, Claude Lefort has put it this way:

> The legitimacy of power is based in the people; but the image of popular sovereignty is linked to *the image of an empty place*, impossible to occupy, such that those who occupy public authority can never claim to appropriate it.[1] (Our emphasis)

Naming and framing the public are central activities of contemporary, mediatized democracies in which the public can only meet itself through representation.

Politicians being interviewed employ the rhetorical device of claiming to understand and stand for "what the public wants". When soap-opera producers construct texts and images intended to depict "ordinary people in real-life situations," when monarchs address people as "my subjects," when racist rabble-rousers insist that they are defending the rights of "us" versus "them," when protest groups make demands in the name of "the silent majority," and when news-readers recite their nightly narratives with a moral inflection that they hope will be acknowledged by "good citizens," they are all engaged in attempts to occupy the empty place in which publics are identified and nurtured.

The aim of this book is to explain how a range of media, from the press to television to the Internet, have constructed and represented the public. We argue that the public is always a product of representation. There is no *a priori* public that is "captured" or "recorded" by the media. The public is invoked through processes of mediation that are dominated by political, institutional, economic, and cultural forces. We explore these processes in the following way. In chapter 1 we consider various ways in which the public (as a social group) and publicness (as a social space) have been historically constructed. We argue that all of these ways are connected by a common thread: the social need to represent mass society by giving witness to the existence of millions of people who, as a collective whole, amount to something qualitatively different from their individual parts. In chapter 2 we develop this historical analysis, relating it to theories of the public sphere. We ask how people come to be addressed as a public and how far members of the public are able to address one another, through the media, on their own terms. In chapter 3 we look at mainstream mass media and their management of public voices through source selection and tight control of occasions in which lay people are allowed to enter their sacred space. In speaking of the mainstream media as a sacred space, we seek to problematize the insider/outsider metaphors which tend to dominate professional media discourse, arguing that the real work of mediation takes place in spaces that are *in between* the institutional media and the represented public. Chapter 4 turns from mainstream to alternative media; from notions of a univocal public to those of pluralistic publics and counterpublics. We discuss examples of mediated self-representations of publics that feel under-represented or misrepresented by the mass media. While recognizing the strength of these independent articulations, we express some concerns about the risk of establishing media enclaves rather than endeavoring to create a pluralistic public sphere in which differences have to be worked through, with all of the communication challenges that entails. Some media theorists regard the Internet as a potential space for such pluralistic, even democratic, interaction. In chapter 5 we question simplistic claims that digital media have disrupted elite dominance of knowledge production and dissemination; enabled anyone to become a media producer; made it easy for people to form and join dispersed communication network which, in turn, can link to other networks; replaced centralized broadcasting by interactive, many-to-many communication channels in which all message senders can expect to receive messages back; and developed online spaces of public deliberation in which positions are not merely articulated and advocated, but revised and even synthesized in response to exposure to others. We argue that there is nothing inevitable or technologically determined about any of these outcomes; that the publicness of the Internet, like other media before it, is subject to contestation at the levels of grass-roots practice as well as policy-making. This leads us to the final chapter, 6, in which we reflect upon the transition from an essentialist and universalist notion of The Public Interest to a more pluralistic conception of publics and their diverse interests. Two conflict-ing roles of the media are considered: on the one hand, a mission to cultivate normatively conceived publics and on the other a duty to be democratically accountable to publics as they constitute themselves. It is this latter role that most media organizations now see themselves performing. They claim to be facilitating discourses between publics with a view to generating the closest possible social connection between them. This is a worthwhile ambition for the media in democratic societies, and we conclude this book by outlining four ways in which the mediated public can make its presence felt and hold power to account: through calls for attention; forms of common sense-making; the generation of public opinion; and the cultivation of civic efficacy. Our conclusion is agenda-setting, but not vigorously prescriptive: our aim is to start and add to debates about the relationship between the media and the public rather than produce a manifesto.

As a key theme explored in this book is the mediation of the public and publics, we have taken seriously, and are intellectually indebted to Thompson's conception of "mediated publicness":

> Actions or events can acquire a publicness which is independent of their capacity to be seen or heard directly by a plurality of co-present individuals. The development of the media has thus given rise to new forms of "mediated publicness" which have assumed an increasingly important role in the modern world.[2]

To be public, in the sense used in this book, is to be open to witness. The public are those who can be witnessed. The public is the space in which witnessing can take place. Conversely, one is a private being – a solely personal actor – when one's actions cannot be witnessed by others. The private sphere is the domain in which one can only be witnessed by intimate observers. Mediation is central to definitions of the public and publicness because it provides and describes the terms of social witnessing. To see the public is to enter a mediated world.

The twenty-first-century public witnesses itself more than any public in history – in vox pops, phone-ins, studio-audience discussions, soap-opera dramatizations, reality TV formats – but it does not control its own image. The mediated public is vulnerable to misrepresentation by media images that fail to reflect its diversity and complexity. Television, for example, is an industry in which certain perspectives are more dominant than others. As most media controllers and senior producers are white, male, and middle class, it is hardly surprising that they are often accused of not understanding sections of the public whose experiences are very different from their own. The media have been accused of misrepresenting a range of social groups: young people, the elderly, the disabled, ethnic minorities, gays, and lesbians, strikers . . . In fact, the empirical evidence on media representations of socio-demographic groups suggests that most people have good reason to complain about the way that people like them are depicted on television. Not only in depicting individuals does television often resort to caricature, but also in the account it gives of the public at large, which is all too often reduced to an inchoate mass. Like a Greek chorus, members of the public are set up to provide background noises consistent with the mood and message of a particular program. In comedies they laugh; in sporting events they cheer; in religious services they close their eyes and pray; in the presence of celebrities they gasp in admiration or sigh in disbelief; in the presence of politicians they often sigh in disbelief, sometimes close their eyes and rarely gasp in admiration. As the media lens provides ever more vivid and revealing close-ups of the once great and distant, its images of the public remain cartoon-like in their linear simplicity.

Consider, for example, this second picture. We have chosen it to contrast with the one at the head of this introduction. Here neither Obama nor the crowd is distinct. In the first picture, one can sense the politician's eagerness to be understood. His hands are outstretched; his eyes meet those of his challenger. While neither Joe the Plumber nor the surrounding crowd look particularly impressed by this human encounter, one can see that they are engaged in something resembling a conversation. In the picture below Obama, though present, is mainly witnessed as an image on a plasma screen. The audience is witnessing his mediated presence – a live event which assumes its legitimacy from looking just like a televized production. The audience here have

Figure 2 Obama at an election rally in Grant Park, Chicago, November 4, 2008. Photo © Grant Gochnauer.

no faces, so all the anxieties about their sullenness, incomprehension, or diversity can be easily swept aside. They are, for the purposes of this semiotic construction, an amorphous public standing before one who represents them as a mediated symbol. Their role in this democratic performance is as expressively nuanced as the symbols on the rows of flags that have been carefully placed around them. As a univocal collectivity, they have a role to play and the cameras will be sure to record them performing on cue. One should not blame them for this; nor Obama; nor the political stage managers; nor the television producers for whom this was just another day and another clichéd image of the mediated public. Blame is certainly not the tone of this book. Instead, we are interested in looking more closely at what is represented in these two pictures and exploring whether a democratic space might be found somewhere between them. We want, in other words, to ask whether ways can be found to capture the personal commitments, experiences, anxieties, and hopes suggested by the first picture on a scale represented in the second picture. Given the inherent fragility of all cultural projects built around the pronoun "we," the question of whether the public can come to witness itself in terms that are pluralistic, sensitive, tolerant, confident, and consequential stands as one of the greatest contemporary challenges to face the media.

1

Imagining the Public

In contemporary society, the public has both a ubiquitous and an invisible presence. In its most vigorous form, as the sovereign *demos* of democracy and the ever-demanding consumers of the marketplace, the public demands to be acknowledged, served, appeased, informed, consulted, and respected. While not wielding power itself, the public knows that those who do possess power can only claim legitimacy by speaking in its name and acting in its interests. The inescapable competition of modern society is for the eyes, ears, tastes, and sympathies of the great amorphous public.

Given that the public occupies such an apparently pivotal social position, it is surprising just how uncertain scholars have been about their capacity to define or recognize it:

> Publics have become an essential fact of the social landscape; yet it would tax our understanding to say exactly what they are.[1]

> It is a place, but you can't walk into it, and it is a group of people – a vast group of people – but they never meet. The place and the people are familiar figures, but although you know them well, you have never seen them and you never will, even though you're one of them.[2]

The public has to be invented – or, at least, imagined – before it can be addressed. The sovereign public has been described as a "phantom" of the social imagination (Lippmann), "an idea, a postulate" (Schlegel), a "monstrous nothing" (Kierkegaard), "a ghostly figure, only ever made present through various proxies."[3] Never meeting in one place or speaking with one voice, the public is unable to represent itself. It is doomed to be represented.

Imagining the public is further complicated by the ambivalence of its role as both actor and stage. As social actor, the public comprises the people who make up society – although, as we shall see, not necessarily all the people all the time. As stage, the public refers to a zone of social openness and transparency, as opposed to privacy and exclusion. But here too, the notion of public space is complicated by a distinction between the official realm of "public affairs," which tend to be highly regulated, and the inclusive public sphere which concerns everyone by virtue of its embeddedness in the daily routines of everyday life. Given these disconcerting ambiguities, it is the aim of this opening chapter to explore the various ways in which the public is imagined, as both a social actor and a social space.

The Public as Social Actor

The roaring public

In recent years, television audiences have been invited to observe a curious weekly ritual in which the inhabitants of the *Big Brother* house await the judgment of the voting public that will lead to the inevitable eviction – from the house, the show, and the passage to celebrity status – of the least popular housemate. It is a climactic moment of tension in which, as Scannell has observed, "two different temporalities encounter each other: time-in-the-house and time-in-the-world."[4] The voters' verdict is announced by the celebrity presenter who, in the fashion of a children's game, instructs evictees to leave the house with the words "I'm coming to get you!" The evictee leaves to re-enter worldly time, at which point the remaining housemates perform a bizarre but functional ritual: they go to the outer wall of their televized enclosure and contort themselves into positions that will enable them to hear the roar of the crowd. The volume, tone, and message of this roar are then discussed for hours, sometimes days. The remote and disembodied voice of the crowd is their only access to the world beyond their voluntary incarceration. It is their one remaining witness to the elusive barometer of public opinion.

The *Big Brother* crowd, which assembles each Friday night in the hope of being seen on television and immersing itself in the drama of a rarely popular electoral event, is neither the mass public that watches the show nor a representative sample of those who voted in the electoral popularity contest. It is a random, symbolic chorus which exists to articulate the mood of public opinion. Its presence indicates that people resembling the millions of domestic viewers are "there" in real time; that the televized event has a live – and living – element. Compare it with election night coverage on the BBC: screens filled with anxious, ambitious, professional politicians, suited players of the game (counters, campaigners, commentators), but hardly a voter to be seen. The *Big Brother* crowd serves as a surrogate embodiment of the public. The incarcerated housemates must press their flesh to the closest possible point of contact with it and interpret its mysterious chants, cheers, and condemnations, just as politicians must spend much of their lives listening out for the murmurs and roars of the public they claim to represent.

Crowds do not have a good historical reputation. As McClelland notes, the record of crowd behavior is dominated by a series of distinctly malignant images:

> the crowd hounding Christ to his death; the crowd bawling for blood in the circus; crowds of mutinous legionaries looking round for someone to raise to the purple . . . Roman mobs making trouble for popes; medieval crowds volatile at great festivals and fairs . . . the barbarism of crowds during the Wars of Religion; Wilkite and Church and King mobs in London; liberty mobs in Boston; the crowd in the French Revolution; lynch mobs; the mobs of industrial discontent.[5]

All of these images have contributed to theories of crowd psychopathology, first articulated in the writings of Taine and Carlyle and subsequently synthesized in the populist account of Le Bon. Taine argued that crowds are characterized by "a steady substratum of brutality and ferocity, and of violent and destructive instincts,"[6] while Carlyle regarded the crowd as comprising "wild inarticulate souls, struggling there, with inarticulate uproar, like dumb creatures in pain, unable to speak what is in them."[7] Few writers have been less sympathetic to crowds than the novelist, George Gissing, who described the 1887 street celebrations for Queen Victoria's Jubilee as "the most gigantic organised exhibition of fatuity, vulgarity, and blatant blackguardism on record" and puts into

the mouth of his protagonist, Piers Otway, in *The Crown of Life* the assertion that "at its best" the crowd is "a smiling simpleton; at its worst,
a murderous maniac."[8] Gustave Le Bon's characterization of crowds
has served as the leading articulation of this tradition:

> Whoever be the individuals that compose it, however like or unlike be
> their mode of life, their occupations, their character, or their intelligence,
> the fact that they have been transformed into a crowd puts them in
> possession of a sort of collective mind which makes them feel, think, and
> act in a manner quite different from that in which each individual of
> them would feel, think, and act were he in a state of isolation.[9]

The image of the crowd as united by unarticulated emotions, intolerant
of individual thought, prone to manipulation by demagogic rabble-
rousers, and incapable of distinguishing between collective fantasy and
reality has prevailed in modern times as a source of elitist fear as well
as a justification for authoritarian control of public gatherings.

Nineteenth-century legislation was dedicated to maintaining order
by preventing the gathering of crowds. In 1817 the British Parliament
passed the Six Acts which required the organizer of any public meeting
to notify the local magistrate at least five days before it was held; for-
bade non-local people from attending such gatherings; and threatened
those assembling without permission with a penalty of seven years'
transportation. Defending the Act in Parliament, Lord Castlereagh
asserted that

> Any assembly of the people, whether armed or unarmed, whether using
> or threatening to use force, or not doing so, and whether the avowed object
> was illegal or legal, if held in such numbers, or with such language
> or emblems, or deportment, as to create well-grounded terror in the
> King's liege subjects for their lives, their persons or their property, was
> an illegal assembly and might be dispersed as such.[10]

This strategy of dispersal was typical of the pre-democratic approach of
governments confronted by visible publics. The Chartists, who campaigned
for universal male suffrage, regarded the spectacle of the gathered
crowd as a symbol of a *demos* in waiting. To gather in vast numbers was
to claim legitimacy as a public demanding acknowledgment. As one
Chartist put it, "What is visible in the streets . . . is only a representative tranche of what lies beyond: the threat is not so many thousand

massed bodies, but so many millions of potential voters here signified corporeally."[11] Plotz has argued in his excellent analysis of Chartist crowd strategies that the movement's decision to hold simultaneous meetings in different parts of the country served to indicate its strength and transformed it from a dispersible crowd into a homogenous public.[12] For once a gathering expands from rooted place to diasporic space it ceases to be a crowd and becomes a public, its character defined not by its physical, but by its social presence. As Dayan and Katz have argued, some publics do congregate, but that is not their defining feature. Crowds must be congregative, or they stop being crowds."[13]

Even after universal male franchise was granted, there were pervasive elite fears of the crowd-like propensities of the newly empowered public. The introduction of the secret ballot, far from simply being a means of protecting voters from intimidation, could be interpreted as a technique of crowd control, designed to prevent the gathering together of the newly enfranchised public. The great Victorian journalist and constitutionalist Walter Bagehot, for example, declared that he was "exceedingly afraid of the ignorant multitude of the new constituencies" and warned that "massing men in concourses" could give rise to "wild excitement among the ignorant poor, which, if once roused, may not be calmed."[14]

The increased sophistication and reach of mass mediation within the past century has made it easy to transmit messages to spatially dispersed publics. More than any previous medium, television enables the public to see itself. Crowds which once took to the streets now head towards the cameras. Public opinion, to be taken seriously, must be registered and graphically displayed via television, although the Internet is now also a significant space of mediated publicity. Appeals to the public by political leaders are made through press releases which compete for media attention and staged interviews in which they pose as ventriloquists of the public's true voice. Witnessing public events is increasingly vicarious: what we believe we have seen for ourselves, we have in fact been shown.

For members of the public seeking to advocate a cause, be it opposition to an unpopular law, an unjust war or the local presence of an alleged child molester, gathering as a crowd is often a first move in setting out a claim to represent the public. Like the Chartists, such campaigns seek to assert their authenticity by mounting a symbolic display of looking and sounding as if they were the public as a whole. When, for example, Chinese students took to the streets to demand the acceleration of the political reforms initiated by the mysteriously deceased Communist Party Secretary, Hu Yaobang, in April 1989, their actions were directed towards the mediated public, reachable through global television, as much as to a domestic Chinese audience. Their banners were written in English; they took advantage of the media corps that had come to Beijing to provide satellite coverage of the state visit of Mikhail Gorbachev; their symbolic use of the "Goddess of Democracy" statue, erected in Tiananmen Square on May 30, 1989, was intended to resonate with Western values of freedom. The mediatized crowd, which is no longer rooted in space or time, depends upon satellites rather than soapboxes for its impact.

The measured public

The specter of the autonomously mobilized multitude led pre-democratic governments to adopt strategies of repressive legislation, intended to prevent or defuse crowd formation. When these did not work, they introduced pacifying reforms, aimed at appeasing the menacing anger of discontented urban crowds. While both of these strategies constituted a response to the immediate threat of crowd disorder, neither provided a sustainable technique for managing the diffuse opinions of the dispersed public. It was the recognition of this task that gave rise to the concept of public opinion.

To imagine public opinion is to envisage the possibility of a homogenous public which can be made visible. The two historical conditions which made this possible were the development of techniques of quantification, by which vast populations could be counted, categorized, and regulated, and democratic politics, the legitimacy of which depended upon the counting in of the public. As Rose has argued,

> Democratic power is calculated power, and numbers are intrinsic in the forms of justification that give legitimacy to political power in democracies. Democratic power is calculating power, and numbers are integral to the technologies that seek to give effect to democracy as a particular set of mechanisms of rule.[15]

Ironically, one of the first exercises in systematic opinion quantification was developed in the early decades of the twentieth century in order to estimate the size of physically gathered crowds.[16] It was the transition from this place-based quantification to attempts to measure the elusive thoughts of dispersed citizens that gave rise to the emergence of public opinion polling in the 1930s. Pioneers such as Gallup believed that scientific sampling techniques could test "the pulse of democracy" by asking questions to "representative" population groups as if they were the public at large. The history of opinion polling over the past 80 years has constituted a striking attempt to attribute ideas to the public in ways that are discrete and cohesive, descriptive and predictive, illuminating and shaming. The public cannot appeal against misrepresentative claims about its opinions, for opinion polling not only defines such opinions but appears to define the public itself. In short, the public's scientifically measured presence has come to be regarded as a more legitimate reality than its autonomous attempts to speak for itself. The crowd came to be seen as wholly observable, explicable, and pre-dictable. As Auden's famous poem, "The Unknown Citizen" suggests, the point of opinion research is to ensure that the public is known better to the government than to itself.

On election-night results' programs the pollsters' "exit polls" precede news of the actual results of legally cast votes – and when the two do not tally media-hired experts are invited to pontificate at length (often self-servingly, for their expertise is intimately related to the legitimacy of the exit polls) about how the public has voted anomalously. For example, approximately 66 million US television viewers watched the third Obama–McCain debate in the run-up to the 2008 presidential election. After the debate was over CNN had a studio packed with pundits, there to tell the viewers what they'd really seen. The overall verdict of the experts was that McCain was the winner on points. Then came the result of a flash poll of Ohio swing voters, conducted online seconds after the debate ended. They pronounced Obama the clear winner. This left the pundits in a peculiar position, predicting an effect that had already happened in their absence and contrary to their judg-ment. In the past, opinion polls had followed the media-driven "debate about the debates"; public opinion was often little more than an echo of expert punditry. Now that technology has made it possible for public opinions to be captured prior to expert exposure, the impression that an authentic, uncontaminated public voice is somehow being assembled enhances the status of the opinion poll as an x-ray of the public mind.

While the value of opinion survey research as a crude method for identifying snapshot responses by selected subjects to carefully framed questions should be acknowledged, the scientific claims of the pollsters should not be accepted uncritically. Following the critiques of Blumer and Bordieu, the extent to which opinion polling is a study of an objectively existing reality should be questioned.[17] Verba's assertion that "surveys give the researcher access to the 'public,' an otherwise broad, amorphous, and hard-to-deal-with phenomenon"[18] is typical of claims made for polling as an inclusive and incisive tool for extracting and aggregating public opinion. We would argue that polls are always discursively situated, constitutive techniques which do not merely capture pre-existing opinion, but conjure it into existence. In other words, what political scientists refer to as "public opinion" is in fact what pollsters decide to poll. A sceptical view of the so-called neutral scientificity of opinion surveys accords with our constructivist conception of the public. Furthermore, Ginsberg's claim that polls allow "governments a better opportunity to anticipate, regulate, and manipulate popular attitudes"[19] and Tilly's observation that social surveys were invented so that "the wealthy and powerful" could "know the nature of the beast that now roared below"[20] help to reveal the sense in which opinion research is an essentially political project. These critics of opinion survey research are not concerned to highlight its methodological shortcomings or even to reject pollsters' capacity to illuminate trends, but to question the very project of seeking a set of opinions which can be attributed to the public as a collective actor. The search for public opinion is never neutral; like all social techniques, it is prompted by particular intentions which are often left unstated.

The motivation for measuring public opinion, we would argue, is anxiety within governing elites. When those who exercise political authority know what they want to do and how to do it, and when they believe that they can do as they wish without provoking the presence of disruptive crowds, there is no need to solicit public opinion. On settled issues of normalized and routinized social practice (companies making profits, children being educated in schools, animals being killed for human consumption), there is no need to resort to the court of public opinion. The jury is brought in when issues are unsettled. To quote Rose once again, "where mistrust of authority flourishes, where experts are the target of suspicion and their claims are greeted with scepticism by politicians, disputed by professional rivals, distrusted by public opinion, where decisions are contested and discretion is criticized, the allure of numbers increases."[21] In short, the counting of the public serves as a court of appeal, whereby unsettled socio-political claims are tested. But not all unsettled claims are tested in this way, for not everyone has access to the technologies of public opinion polling or the means of authoritatively disseminating the results of such measurement. Just as crowds must appeal to the media to be acknowledged, numbers carry little weight until they are reported in a certain voice: the tone of the scientifically incontrovertible; the measured voice of one who has the measure of the inchoate public.

It should be noted that opinion polling has not been the only route of access to the thoughts and experiences of the public. In the same decade that Gallup established the American Institute of Public Opinion, a rather different, more qualitative approach to the capture of the public mood was initiated in the UK by Madge, Harrison, and Jennings, the founders of the Mass Observation research movement. Mass Observation used a team of volunteer field-workers to engage in indirect observation, direct interviews, and survey production in order to create accounts of everyday conversations about issues of the day, ranging from the Coronation of King George VI in 1937 to clothes-rationing. As well as issue-based studies, Mass Observation was interested in human interactions within popular cultural settings, such as pubs, cinemas, and shops. From these field studies, which Mass Observation referred to as an "anthropology of ourselves," they aimed to produce what they called a "weather map of popular feeling." Madge and Harrison were of the view that the media were failing to reflect the thoughts and feelings of the public. Mass Observation has been described as an attempt "to socialise the means of documentary production by providing ordinary people with a channel through which they could communicate what went on around them, within the ambit of their day-to-day lives."[22] Rejecting quantitative research methods, Mass Observation sought to capture the mood of the public through a montage of documentary-like observations and almost poetically structured impressionism. The demise of Mass Observation occurred when it moved towards a more managed approach to opinion-gathering, first during World War II when it agreed to be commissioned by the Ministry of Information to produce "morale reports" on the state of public feeling, and then after the war, when it constructed increasingly "narrowly focused surveys for commercial companies with products to sell, such as its surveys on washing habits, on the domestic use of paint and on the public taste for cosmetics, custard powder, baked beans and frozen fish."[23]

By 1949 the original movement was superseded by Mass Observation Ltd., which was effectively a commercial market-research company. Nonetheless, in the decade after 1937 Mass Observation produced over 20 published volumes from which a remarkable qualitative account of contemporary publics, if not *the* public, could be derived.

Post-war political journalism has been increasingly dominated by apparent evidence from opinion polls, as if these are the only means of sensing public consciousness, prompting some commentators to describe the media coverage of US presidential campaigns as "a poll orgy." Reports of polls are often confusing and contradictory in terms of identifying public opinion, especially when read against the less frequent people-on-the-street interviews which offer a more nuanced picture. The establishment of such a complex picture – not in the mimetic sense of capturing a pre-existing reality, but of enabling publics to emerge in ways that reflect the affects and ambiguities of quotidian speech – entails a movement away from the simplistic claims of polling research to "reveal" the public by reducing it to mere data.

The attentive public

Thus far we have conceptualized the public as a source – of threatened disorder, in the case of crowds, and of scientifically ascertainable opinion in the case of polling. A third way to think about the public is as an active recipient of messages. The geographer, Clive Barnett, has defined the public as "the figure for the uncertain addressee of communicative acts oriented towards universality."[24] In this sense, the public is not a fixed, objective reality, but a way of speaking to strangers with whom one needs to share social space. When Queen Elizabeth II, in her annual Christmas speech, addresses "her" public, she is, in one sense, taking a gamble that the recipients of her message are (a) listening to her and (b) prepared to accept this definition of themselves within the ecology of British social power. When the government of North Korea at one time paid for the regular placement of full-page advertisements in broadsheet British newspapers, explaining how Kim-Il-Sung had been misrepresented by the Western media and was in fact the defender of the "proletarian masses," it assumed (mistakenly, as it turns out) that an attendant public would emerge and then act in some way upon its message.

In his seminal work on publics and counterpublics, Warner argues that for an appeal to be made to the public it must be impersonally addressed to strangers, while at the same time personally addressed to putative fellow citizens: "Public speech can have great urgency and intimate import. Yet we know that it was addressed not exactly to us but to the stranger we were until the moment we happened to be addressed by it."[25] The suggestion here is that the public comes into being dynamically, through historical action, rather than ontologically, as an essential social form. "The existence of a public is contingent on its members' activity, however notional or compromised, and not on its members' categorical classification, objectively determined position in the social structure, or material existence."[26]

Appeals to the public are predicated, therefore, upon expectations about what that public will be like once it is formed. Such expectations are not always met, for actual, historical publics can be creative and recalcitrant in determining their own lifeworld. Nonetheless, these formative anticipations (which Warner refers to as "the poetic function of public discourse"[27]) are critical to the emergence and definition of publics. For example, nation-states address their citizens not only as a public, but as a distinctly characterized and normatively admissible public. When the US President speaks to "my fellow Americans" he is not only claiming that a public which will recognize itself as "fellow Americans" exists and will hear him, but that they are of a specific, historical texture that will respond to his words in predictable and approved ways. Of course, this does not always happen when leaders address their followers, as was witnessed when the Romanian president, Nicolae Ceaușescu, addressed "his public" on December 21, 1989 and they began by booing and ended by executing him. All attempts to connect with a public entail the risk of rejection. Public communication is inherently promiscuous, insofar as any appeal to the public necessarily abandons "the security of [a] positive, given audience" and "commits itself in principle to the possible participation of any stranger."[28] It is the discourse of the soapbox on a street corner, where words must be directed to whoever happens to be passing by, rather than the gentleman's club, where everyone knows everyone else.

Thinking of the public as a product of social circulation is helpful in countering notions of the public as a pre-existing entity waiting to be discovered. It enables us to think of the public as a mediated presence which emerges, atrophies, and reforms in response to a diverse array

of messages directed towards it. As a ceaselessly risky ecology of anticipations, avoidances, silences, connections, and miscommunications,
public culture can never be relied upon, but forever tested by verbal and
semiotic gestures designed to secure its attention.

Nothing embodies this ongoing testing more vividly than media
ratings systems, devised to estimate the percentage of people or households in a given market exposed to a particular channel, station,
program, or newspaper. Ratings have come to dominate mainstream
media production at every level, treating audiences, like publics, as tar-
gets of attention. Whereas public opinion pollsters claim to measure the
outcome of attention, media ratings systems measure attention itself.

> Basically, it is people's shared orientation toward some focal point – a
> centre of transmission, a centre of attraction – that turns them into
> "audience members." In this context, the idiosyncrasies of the individual
> people making up an audience, as well as the specific interrelations
> between these people, do not matter: audience as taxonomic collective
> is in principle a term of amassment.[29]

What, we might ask, is the difference between an audience, as collective beholders of a spectacle, and publics? If the principal function of the
public is to receive messages, it becomes difficult to distinguish between
the viewer – especially the active viewer of recent reception theory –
and the citizen – especially the apathetic citizen lamented by political
commentators. As Livingstone has suggested, "Instead of bemoaning the
impact of media on publics, let us ask how media (and media audiences)
can and do sustain publics."[30] Suggestive as this argument may be,
there remains a strong sense in which it leaves thinking, experiencing,
imagining human beings with too little work to do. Just as the imagined
crowd is required only to congregate and make a noise and the public
whose opinions are polled are required to report their views to experts
without having to act upon them, the attendant, message-receiving
public is in one sense little more than a stake in a speculation about
the potential effects of publicity. As an historical force, it lacks the kind
of agency that the humanist Enlightenment celebrated in its project
to bring "things into such a shape that the members of the human
species will no more be thwarted in their urge to act according to the most
human of their natural endowments: the power to pass rational judgement and behave according to the precepts of reason."[31] Embodying

these highest attributes of humanity, the Enlightenment public was conceived as a rationally and ethically discriminating social actor whose role was to pursue its own emancipation from mystery and falsification. Although twentieth-century history dented such confidence in the public's capacity for self-emancipatory virtue and the dehumanizing experiences of Fascism and Stalinism encouraged an intellectual retreat into caricatures of the fickle, malleable, and ultimately reckless public, there remains one role that cannot be abstracted from collective humanity: that of the historical witness.

The witnessing public

The emergence of both mass society and technologies of mass communication in the past 150 years have led us to depend more than ever before upon a particular kind of moral and political force: the power of public witnessing. As Ellis has rightly observed, "We know more and have seen more of this century than the generations of any previous century knew or or saw of theirs . . . Certainly, 'I did not know' and 'I did not realize' are not open to us as a defence."[32]

Of course, witnessing has always been a vital element in human activity and reflexivity. The role of the witness is central to any conception of justice. Even before secular governance became prevalent, the witnessing of miracles, divine presence, and moral retribution were regarded as essential public functions. To give witness, in the sense of translating the sensation of direct observation into words or images that can be shared by others who then become vicariously complicit in an indirect experience, is what makes humans historically conscious animals. "Witnesses," argues Peters, "serve as the surrogate sense-organs of the absent."[33] Witnesses are also time-travellers, transmitting the past into the present and the present into the future. While such witnessing has always constituted a dimension of public culture, it has only been in the past 150 years that technologies of mass witnessing have come to play a central role in determining and disseminating historical and political reality. The public as witness of its own history has come to be a defining characteristic of late modernity.

In one sense, the witnessing public is a response to the processes whereby our different worlds are increasingly sharing the same single space. This process is closely related to the compression and separation of global time and space which Giddens refers to as "time-space distanciation":

> In conditions of late modernity we live "in the world" in a different sense from previous eras of history. Everyone still continues to live a local life, and the constraints of the body ensure that all individuals, at every moment, are contextually situated in time and space. Yet the transformations of place, and the intrusion of distance into local activities, combined with the centrality of mediated experience, radically change what "the world" actually is.[34]

It is impossible to live in the globalized world without depending upon events, information, and expertise which originate from far away. We cannot hope to rely upon direct, sensual experience as our principal means of accessing the world. The strangers who are our fellow citizens are mainly people we will never meet; the news that makes and shakes our world might take place thousands of miles away, but it will still have major local ramifications. The local is increasingly lived under the shadow of the global. In such circumstances, the "we" who constitute the public is widely dispersed and dependent for self-knowledge upon mediated and indirect accounts of itself. Only through technologies of mediated witnessing can publics emerge and come to know themselves. From "reality TV" depictions of "ordinary" and "extraordinary" people to YouTube videos of war zones and exotic practices, there prevails a common rhetoric of witnessing, seeming to say "Look at this; for in doing so, you will come to know yourself better." As we shall argue in subsequent chapters, both mainstream and alternative media are tied into an ongoing battle to characterize the public; to make particular accounts of the public familiar while marginalizing others. Claims by media producers to get close to, reflect vividly, or even embody the real cannot be separated from the competing intentions, strategies, and deceptions inherent to this battle to characterize the public.

The Public as Social Space

As well as referring to an historical actor, the term "public" also describes a set of spatial relations within which social action takes place. Public space should not be understood in a narrowly topological sense, as a physically dimensional place, but as a social configuration comprising practiced and experienced relationships of interaction. As Kohn states, "Spatial configurations naturalize social relations by transforming contingent forms into a permanent landscape that appears as immutable rather than open to contestation."[35] In recent years social theory has been influenced considerably by what has been called a "spatial turn," which describes a broad set of enquiries related to the production and significance of space. Foucault and his adherents have attempted to show how the design and management of space constitute primary instruments of social control, as in the case of panoptic architecture which exposes all social action to the surveillant gaze of authorities.[36] Others argue that spatial practices can be emancipatory as well as disciplinarian, and have undertaken research into specific spaces of transformative micropower. Key to such investigations are distinctions between public and private space.

Private space is closed off, invisible to outsiders, and governed by internally specific rules. The most typical example of a private space is the home – and within the home there are spaces that are particularly private, such as bedrooms and toilets. These are reserved spaces in which certain forms of behavior are shielded from public view. Such behavior is often described as "personal," insofar as it is not the business of the public. In recent years, however, this rigid distinction between the personal affairs of private life and the wider domain of public affairs has been open to critical question. A number of people, particularly feminists, have argued that "the personal is political" and that intimate relationships that were once considered inviolably private – such as those between parents and children, or between sexual partners – should be open to public debate, and even interference if they are deemed to be exploitative or harmful. While the boundaries between public and private have become blurred in ways that would shock a time-traveller from the nineteenth century, they persist as the most significant categories of contemporary social life. Even in the age of Big Brother and *Big Brother*, in which there is one CCTV camera in the UK for every 14 British citizens and in which permanent surveillance has become a major feature of reality TV, vulnerable distinctions remain between public and private spaces. Three defining characteristics of public space are of particular significance: accessibility, universality, and visibility.

Accessibility

Public space is open for all to enter. While often governed by constraining rules of conduct, such spaces are defined by allowing unrestricted
access and rights of way. For example, parks are public spaces because
anyone can enter them, without distinction of status, wealth, or beliefs.
Non-tangible public spaces are also characterized by their accessibility,
such as the expectation in democracies that the legal system should
be open to all – not just physical places, like police stations and courts,
but intangible aspects of legality, such as rights, judicial precepts, and
the language of the law. In practice, such public spaces might not be as
accessible as they purport to be, but they are at least open to criticism
for failing to meet generally agreed standards of openness. In contrast,
private spaces, such as boardrooms or bedrooms, are not open to criticism for excluding the public.

Because accessibility is a defining feature of public spaces, attempts
to exclude people from them often results in contestation. Mitchell's case
study of the battle to retain free access to People's Park in Berkeley,
California, provides an excellent example of how "by claiming space
in public . . . social groups themselves become public."[37] In this specific
case, an attempt was made to drive homeless people out of a park
that had hitherto been open to an inclusive public. By redefining the
terms of spatial inclusion, the homeless were effectively excluded from
membership of the public. The battle to keep the park open to all was
not simply about the governance of a particular place, but the nature
of the public, both spatially and civically.

In an earlier episode, the Reform League demanded the right for
citizens to assemble in Hyde Park, London, to discuss reform of the
franchise. The League, which had 600 branches, called a mass meeting
in Hyde Park for July 2, 1866. Sir Robert Mayne, the Superintendent
of the Metropolitan Police, at first banned the gathering, but then
relented and a crowd of 50,000 people assembled. A further meeting
was planned for July 23, but this time the Home Secretary, Spencer
Walpole, issued a ban on "meetings for the purpose of delivering or
hearing speeches, or for the public discussion of popular and exciting
topics."[38] On July 23, Hyde Park was surrounded by 17,000 police, but
the crowd outnumbered them and broke through the railings, forcing
their way into the park. According to the next day's press report, the

police responded with ferocity: "Wherever there was a skull to fracture, they did their best to fracture it; everybody was in their eyes an enemy to whom no mercy was to be shown."[39] Nonetheless, the crowd stayed in the park and returned on the two following days to make speeches and assert their right of access to an acknowledged public space. On July 28, the Government's law officers declared that it was "impractical" to prevent people from meeting in the park. Nonetheless, a further Hyde Park meeting, planned for May 6, 1867, was banned by Walpole, who explained to Parliament the danger of allowing gatherings about issues "on which men's minds are easily excited."[40] The government was supported by the opposition leader, Gladstone, who declared that "the scum of this great city would take advantage of such an assemblage."[41] Despite such rhetoric, on the day the police were unable to uphold the ban: 15,000 people entered the park, ignoring the police, and Walpole resigned as Home Secretary the following day. In 1872 the Park Regulation Act was passed, allowing anyone to hold a meeting in Hyde Park without prior permission. A civic right had been asserted. (Speakers still gather in Hyde Park every Sunday.)

The concept of citizenship is intimately related to conditions of spatial accessibility, for civic behavior depends upon a series of rights of entry, ranging from the polling station to town squares to cyberspace where much contemporary interaction now occurs. In the absence of these rights of public access, democratic citizenship becomes a pious aspiration rather than a practicable commitment.

Universality

Public space is universal rather than particular. It is a realm of impersonal relations, in which the safe familiarity of mutual recognition gives way to the fleeting acknowledgments of passing strangers. In this sense, that which is public is broad and fragile: available to all and any, but lacking any firm right to attention. Unlike private and personal affairs, which appeal to self-interest and purposeful curiosity, public affairs are often regarded with indifference, as the remote workings of a self-generating and self-serving system. Linking the collective priorities of impersonal public space to the private passions of biographical existence is perhaps the most challenging task of mass societies.

But first societies must determine what is appropriately public and what is not. These are fluid categories. Once strictly privatized, intimate matters, such as sexual orientation and attachment, have become matters of public experience and debate. At the same time, spaces that were once regulated in the name of public vigilance, such as vote-casting and film-watching, are increasingly migrating to domestic privacy. Matters are made universal through claims that they relate to everyone and made non-public when such claims are rejected.

Publics, comprising strangers who might not ordinarily meet, can only form if spaces exist in which heterogeneous encounters can take place and be developed. Before anything resembling democracy can be said to exist, inclusive public spaces have to be established, for, as Hannah Arendt argued, "before men began to act, a definite space had to be secured and structure built where all subsequent actions could take place."[42] Public space is where ideas, issues, and dilemmas relevant to anyone and everyone can circulate over time. This conception of communication as a circulatory process – a series of interactions over time between claims and attention – is helpful in understanding the notion of universalistic public space. It is what Anderson had in mind when he wrote about the invention of the printing press and the spread of vernacular texts giving rise to the "imagined communities" of European nation states.[43] Similarly, one might argue that it was the *circulation* of early news-papers, with their reports of trading voyages, foreign adventures, and price fluctuations, that gave rise to a consciousness of the universal significance of global market relationships.

In the context of democratic political relationships, which depend for their health upon vibrant public spaces of interaction, universality is tested and played out within what has become known as the public sphere. According to Kant, ideas can only be effectively tested if they are exposed to public reason.[44] As spaces of socially cross-cutting intellectual exposure such as coffee-houses and salons emerged, the possibility of an inclusive public conversation was raised. Habermas, who has famously discussed the history and democratic functions of the public sphere, states that "The public sphere can best be described as a network for communicating information and points of view (i.e. opinions expressing affirmative or negative attitudes); the streams of communication are, in the process, filtered and synthesised in such a way that they coalesce into bundles of topically specified public opinions."[45] There has been a tendency to over-institutionalize Habermas's account of the public sphere, confining it to "official" spaces, such as the press, television, or political parties. In contrast, Negt and Kluge counter the depiction of the public sphere as comprising "a few professionals," such as "politicians, editors, officials or federations" and argue that a truly public sphere "has to do with everybody" and "is only realized in the heads of people, as a dimension of their consciousness."[46] Unlike private affairs, which resist the interference of outsiders, public affairs are of universal relevance and circulate within spaces from which nobody can be justifiably excluded. The unprecedented public debate about the Iraq war is a good example of an issue which "has to do with everybody." Some politicians, military strategists, diplomats, or embedded journalists might claim to have special insights into the justice of this war, but the ethos of universality upon which the democratic public sphere is founded affords just as much legitimacy to returning soldiers, parents of combatants, peace campaigners, and interested citizens as it does to elites seeking to speak for the public. The health of the public sphere is tested by its capacity to provide room for all voices, regardless of their status, background, or mode of expression.

Visibility

But before public space can be accessible or deemed to be of universal relevance, it must be visible to all. As Thompson has explained, "What is public . . . is what is visible or observable, what is performed in front of spectators, what is open for all or many to see or hear or hear about."[47] Whereas it was once the case that social power was protected by seclusion and opacity, in democratic societies there is an expectation that power should be visible for all to witness and scrutinize.

The case of Parliament, as the center of representative power in Britain, provides a useful illustration. During its long period as an institution that was dominated by a patrician elite, there existed no principle of accountability to the governed. For example, in 1571, Members of Parliament resisted the publication of verbatim report of the proceedings of Parliament and penalized reporters who attempted to publish such material, arguing that "every person of the Parliament ought to keep secret and not to disclose the secrets and things done and spoken in Parliament House to any other person, unless he be one of the same House, upon pain of being sequestered out of the House, or otherwise punished as by order of the House shall be appointed."[48] It was not until 1878 that a Select Committee examined the question of allowing an official report of the proceedings of the House of Commons to be produced, and it was not until 1909 that the daily *Hansard* reports were finally declared to be official records, when the *Official Report* was legitimized as a parliamentary service, on the basis that the public, who since 1884 had obtained the right to vote, ought to be free to know what their elected representatives were doing in their name. As Parliament moved from secrecy to visibility, a press lobby was established (1884), radio microphones were allowed in (1978), and cameras were allowed to film the live proceedings of the House of Lords (1985) and then the House of Commons (1989), though in both cases the rules of filming were strictly regulated by Parliament itself. What one sees here is a parallel evolution of democratization and visibility: as Parliament's legitimacy came to depend upon being seen to speak for the public, technologies of public visibility became more important. Indeed, between the early 1930s and the late 1990s, a profound change of perspective in relation to the significance of political visibility had taken place. In 1932, the Speaker of the House of Commons told Parliament that the Prime Minister and others believed it was undesirable for the BBC's press gallery reporters to provide a daily account of the dealings of Parliament. Several decades later, when the BBC was considering program changes, the then Speaker of the House, Betty Boothroyd, hoped that nothing would happen to the one of its flagship programs, *Yesterday in Parliament*, since it performed an important function in bringing Parliament closer to the people. From dependence for its authority upon the maintenance of a dignified distance from the vulgar public, parliamentary power came to depend upon techniques designed to make it appear close and connected to those it claimed to represent.

Thompson[49] has very usefully shown how the nature of public visibility has changed as technologies of mediation have given rise to "a new kind of publicness which consists of . . . *the space of the visible . . .* in which mediated symbolic forms can be expressed and received by a plurality of non-present others." Mediated publicness is experienced through technologies and techniques designed to convey an impression of presence. Television is the most ubiquitous provider of such mediated experiences but, as the word itself suggests, a trade-off is involved. Tele (distance) and vision (seeing) embodies both the promise of mediation – extending visual reach across vast spatial distances – and its inherent compromise between the sensual experiences of direct involvement and the limitations of virtual witnessing. One of the authors recalls well living within walking distance of Wembley Stadium when the 1966 Soccer World Cup Final was played. Watching the momentous last minutes of the match on television, he could hear the gasps and roars of the live crowd as goals were scored and missed. In order to experience the naked reality of the occasion, the television sound had to be turned down so that the immediate (unmediated) vibrations from the stadium could be heard and felt directly. The same gasps and roars were audible from the television set, but these were somehow once removed from the originality that characterizes authentic experience. On occasions such as these, mediation can make spaces public, but cannot necessarily guarantee the quality of such encounters. A key aim of this book is to problematize the sense in which mediation devalues that which it makes available. Specifically, we are interested in ways that the mediated public is both reflected and constituted; represented and reconfigured.

2

Public Spheres

Having argued in the previous chapter that the public has no onto-logical essence prior to mediated representation, we turn in this chapter to an account of how spaces of publicness – or public spheres – have emerged, converged, and atrophied. All public communication in modern, mass societies depends upon mediating technologies, techniques, strategies, and performances. Such patterns of mediation cannot be neatly categorized in ways that make them historically distinct from one another – and this chapter is not an attempt to do so. What follows is not an historical narrative, but a typology of cultural conceptions of mediated publicness. Our aim is to show that *being public* and *making publics* are rooted within historical contexts and characterized by intentions, contingencies, and inconsistencies.

We shall consider three conceptions of the public sphere. The first, following Habermas's early account, constructs the public as a homogeneous entity. Such cohesion is produced at the expense of the non-representation of disruptive social elements, such as foreigners, dissidents, and deviants, who do not accord with the normative charac-teristics of well-governed citizens. A second conception of the public sphere, linked to the rise of broadcasting in the early twentieth century, relies upon an educative strategy, conceiving the public as something to be moulded and tamed. The task of the media is seen as being to provide the public with what it needs, and indeed to reshape its needs so that it wants what is normatively better for it. To be addressed as a public in such a context is to be placed in a status of tutelage, while appar-ently being offered a service. Thirdly, and more recently, conceptions of the public sphere have placed a democratic emphasis upon hearing public voices, "letting the public in" to media spaces and encouraging various forms of active citizenship. The kind of public sphere envisaged here promotes norms of civic participation, with all of the problematic tensions between management and autonomy, self-determination and collusion which that term entails.

Critical Discussion, the Liberal Press, and the Bourgeois Public Sphere

In late seventeenth- and eighteenth-century Europe, the public – which had always existed in one form or another, as slaves, plebeians, peasants, merchants, and artisans – came into its own as a powerful discursive construct. This new public emerged out of the convergence of two fundamental historical changes: the demise of feudal absolutism, in which all had been subjected to the power of the state and all expression displayed one's rank in the social hierarchy; and the rise of the capitalist global market, which opened a creative chasm between state power and private life, thereby allowing new relationships of civic association and consumer choice to flourish. According to Habermas's now famous early account of the bourgeois public sphere, one of its defining characteristics was a new role for the press as "an institution of the public itself, effective in the manner of a mediator and intensifier of public discussion."[1]

Acting as neither an official messenger for the state nor a merely commercial product of consumption, the liberal press, according to Habermas, served as a forum of self-referential discourse in which reflexive public subjectivity laid a foundation for public opinion. Citizens within the public sphere possessed what Habermas has called an "abstract universality": they shared rights, responsibilities, and a collective capacity to enter into reasoned debate about matters of mutual interest and concern. However, this liberal conception of the sovereign public, before which the state and all other powers must stand accountable, was predicated upon the possibility of a univocal mass subject reaching a consensus through rational communication. To exercise its sovereign role, such a mass subject had to be strong enough to overcome whatever fragmented interests and values divided it. As La Vopa has observed, the public was a mysterious, not to say miraculous, phenomenon. Somehow myriad personal judgements, each formed autonomously within the inner sanctum of conscience, cohered into a collective will with a credible claim to rational objectivity.[2]

The ideal of the mass subject came close to Rousseau's myth of the general will: "every individual could hear the voice of all, thus the voice of no one, and could, in the last analysis, believe he was hearing his own voice."[3] This ideal of a homogenous public was indeed a fiction and, empirically, the Habermasian account of the rise of the public has been convincingly challenged by historians who have argued that its focus upon the largely male, bourgeois public of the eighteenth-century salons and coffee-houses is too narrow and exclusive; that it could only be sustained through strategies of representation which have refused to acknowledge the presence of diversity, inequality, and conflict within the actually existing, rather than the ideologically constructed public.

The bourgeois public sphere cracked under two related strains. First, the bourgeois public's sense of itself relied upon a bifurcated perspective, according to which "we, the public" were seen as thoughtful, responsible, law-abiding social stakeholders, while those failing to meet such standards – specifically, the working class – could be justifiably marginalized and excluded from the arena of consequential discussion. This splitting of the public into respectable and unmentionable elements destined the latter to ridicule or disdain; a form of unofficial exile from the claims of public sovereignty which could only be sustained within a pre-democratic polity.

The *bourgeois* public sphere depended upon a way of seeing others that rendered them invisible. Its liberal rhetoric of openness, free speech, and universal reason, which had been progressive in relation to the closed polity of the absolutist state, came in the course of the nineteenth century to be regarded as a mendacious apologia for cultural exclusion.

The second reason for the demise of the bourgeois public sphere relates to the commercially transformative dynamic of the capitalist political economy. Whereas the Habermasian public sphere depended upon a journalistic space that was unencumbered by private interests, by the early nineteenth century media institutions were becoming large-scale businesses delivering news as a commodity with a view to profit. Ownership of the press was consolidated into the hands of business tycoons with little interest in the cultivation of bourgeois chatter.

The new mass audience for journalism, comprising the recently literate and enfranchized, was seen as a market for the transmission of popular messages as well as a public that could be politically shaped.

The Listening Audience and the National Public Sphere

By the early twentieth century the press had become wholly oriented towards commerce. The emergence of public service broadcasting in Britain in the 1920s offered a potential alternative to the privatization of national debate. The establishment of the BBC provided an unprecedented opportunity to address the mass audience for radio, and later television, as if it were a single subject. John (later Lord) Reith, the first Director-General of the BBC, was convinced that the public, as mass audience, could only benefit from receiving forms of information, education, and entertainment that they would not choose for themselves. He believed that the aim of public service broadcasting should be to improve rather than reflect public tastes: "He who prides himself on giving what he thinks the public wants is often creating a fictitious demand for low standards which he will then satisfy."[4] Reith's response to the accusation of "setting out to give the public not what it wanted, but what the BBC thought it should have" was that "few knew what they wanted, fewer what they needed."[5] The task of the public broadcaster was not, therefore, to provide a space in which ordinary people could represent themselves, but to offer a sphere of tutelage in which the public could be represented to itself as it should be. The BBC's declared objective of informing and educating the public was to be carried out in ways that would mold its audience in an appropriate civic fashion, giving them what it believed they needed and telling them what they should want.

The pre-war BBC's intellectual paternalism was exemplified by the productions emanating from its Talks Department, which found itself in the 1920s and 1930s under considerable pressure to "exercise . . . vigilance and discerning judgement" in determining the speakers to whom the listening audience should be exposed.[6] This entailed a strategy of tacit censorship. Efforts were made by the Talks Department to recruit expert commentary from the respectable and edifying middle ground, as opposed to "controversial" or "partial" viewpoints. In effect, this meant selecting speakers whose views on social and cultural matters veered between the worthy and the innocuous. Talks were intended to raise rather than reflect the level of public thinking, and this could only be achieved by establishing norms of "common sense" that were inevitably ideological constructions. Such norms had been worked out during the course of the General Strike of 1926, in which Reith had reassured the government with the rather disingenuous syllogism that "Assuming the BBC is for the people, and that the Government is for the people, it follows that the BBC must be for the Government in this crisis too."[7]

The BBC sometimes behaved in these early days as if it was inventing the public sphere from scratch and inviting its audience to experience the novelty of debating public affairs. For many listeners, exposure to the BBC's controlled discussion contrasted sharply with their experience of vivacious grass-roots discussions in union meetings, pub conversations and street-corner oratory (which still existed in most British towns and cities in the inter-war years). In seeking to install itself within an extant public realm in which matters of common interest were already being discussed, often in inclusive and democratic ways, the BBC was not inventing the public sphere, but seeking to alter the terms of engagement of public discourse by confining the uncultivated public to the role of passive listeners. This approach alienated democratic critics, one of whom argued in a speech in the House of Commons that the BBC was run "very largely by people who do not know the working class, do not understand the working-class point of view, but are seeking evidently to mould the working class."[8]

As a public service broadcaster and principal shaper of the national identity, the Reithian BBC found it hard to resist modes of paternalistic address which operated at three related levels: its tone was impersonal, addressed to an amorphous mass rather than individual, contextually situated recipients; its content was highly managed, with a view to protecting the public from unedifying words, thoughts, and voices; and its conception of serious discourse was narrow, exclusive, and somewhat repressed. The only way that the BBC could avoid this impression of being a voice from above, preaching condescendingly to a largely indifferent public, was by entering into a more sociable relationship with its audience. As the BBC faced up to this task, three stylistic aspirations predominated: the cultivation of new forms of personal address;

the promotion of spontaneous talk; and the opening up of "human" aspects of public affairs.

Mediated sociability entailed moving beyond impersonal modes of address which seemed to regard the audience as an anonymous collectivity. Millions of people had to be spoken to as if they were each the recipient of messages meant for them. Scannell has described this as the movement from *for-anyone* to *for-anyone-as-someone* structures of communication.[9] The for-anyone mode of address regarded the audience as being a crowd in the presence of a great orator. It was the style of the declamatory and commanding megaphone rather than the intimate and soothing microphone. For-anyone was the ethos of industrial mass production, which assumed an inherent estrangement between the conception and the reception of mediated messages. The disembodied nature of mediated communication could not replace for-anyone structures with for-someone structures, for these can only be realized in the context of interpersonal, rather than mass communication. Instead, as Scannell has astutely suggested, the task of the mass media was to construct

> an intermediary structure that mediates between the impersonal for-anyone structure and the personal for-someone structure. As such the for-everyone-as-someone structure expresses and embodies that which is in between the impersonal third person (the me-and-you). The for-everyone-as-someone structure expresses "we-ness."[10]

In seeking to pull off this communicative shift, the BBC could draw for inspiration upon earlier media styles. *Tit-Bits*, the popular magazine established by George Newnes in 1881, was perhaps the original exemplar of a style designed to persuade its mass readership that they were being addressed personally. While magazines had previously aimed to edify and uplift readers deemed to be from the lower orders, *Tit-Bits* invited its readers to relate to it as if they were members of a community: not merely passively receiving the weekly text, but contributing to it through the submission of their own stories about everyday life. *Tit-Bits* addressed its readers as friends and invited them to interact with the magazine through readers' queries, competitions, and insurance schemes. This combination of amicable address and authorial interactivity proved to be immensely popular. With a weekly circulation of around half a million, *Tit-Bits* was by 1893 the world's most popular penny magazine. Its style became known as the New Journalism and came to be widely imitated. For example, *True Story*, launched in 1919, took interactivity even further by inviting readers to send in confessional stories in return for small payments. These stories constituted the main text of the magazine, allowing it to be seen as "a literature produced by people for people with responses published from 'ordinary' people."[11]

But mediated sociability is always constructed around suppositions about who the readers (listeners, viewers) are assumed to be. How do they speak in their own voice and which modes and tones of address are likely to appeal to them? What do they need to understand in order to engage in socially meaningful intercourse? What will they not understand? Answering these questions, often implicitly, but always ideologically, entails an imaginary construction of the public in order to address it in terms of familiarity. Magazines like *Tit-Bits* and *True Story* succeeded not only in appealing to particular publics, but in shaping and giving discrete identity to them.

The task for the BBC was to replicate the sociability of the New Journalism by abandoning its aura of anonymous authority and cultivating a speaking-to-you voice to which listeners could relate individually. The BBC's confidence in its capacity to relate to the public was shaken by its first systematic efforts to find out who its audience was and what it was thinking. The BBC Listener Research Section was established in 1936, under the direction of Robert Silvey, and although Reith insisted that production decisions should under no circumstances be based upon audience demand, knowledge derived from public feedback had an inevitable impact upon the BBC's sense of how it was being received. It became clear from BBC Listener Research reports that particular styles and personalities were popular, while the official voices of BBC authority were unwelcome in people's homes. As the BBC came to understand the domestic context of reception, it acknowledged the necessity of cultivating homely voices which would be regarded by the public as welcome guests. From the mid-1930s the BBC began to promote radio personalities, such as Wilfred Pickles and J.B. Priestley, whose success depended upon the cultivation of relationships of parasocial intimacy with their audiences. Rather than being addressed as an amorphous collectivity, listeners were invited to collude with the new radio personalities to maintain an illusion of private and personal contact, albeit through a public medium. The rehearsed spontaneity of radio talk – Goffman called this "fresh talk"[12] – inspired intense audience loyalty, even though the communicative relationship it depended upon was "one-sided, non-dialectical, controlled by the performer, and not susceptible of mutual development."[13] For the time being, at least, broadcasters had found a voice which seemed to be talking to rather than at ordinary people.

The second task for the BBC was to come to terms with the risks inherent in spontaneous communication. Early BBC talks were, paradoxically, both live and edited. The tyranny of the pre-edited script meant that all BBC talk had to be screened before being uttered. This was a consequence of the Reithian BBC's compulsion to perform an improving role – seeking to edify the public, while obsessively avoiding any risk of controversial content. This could only possibly have led to a narrowing of the rhetorical range, limiting speakers with recognized reputations to the style of the Oxbridge common room, while confining lay contributors to a homely mateyness which smacked of simulation and condescension. For example, in 1931 the BBC launched *Conversations on a Train* which was supposed to capture voices of casual conversation as people as people traveled on trains. The sound effects of a moving train were authentic enough, but the voices were those of professional actors reading scripts! The series was eventually taken over by the BBC's Drama Department.[14]

When unorthodox speakers were given the privilege of access to the BBC microphones, they were expected to collude with a system of editorial censorship designed to produce anodyne content and artificial style. In some cases this went badly wrong, as when the communist, William Ferrie, was invited to present a talk as part of a 1933 BBC series on *The National Character.* Ferrie submitted his script to the producers who were of the view that several parts of it – about working-class exploitation and the trickery of calls for a national effort to increase production – were irrelevant to the subject of the series. Ferrie apparently agreed to his talk being edited, but when he appeared before the microphone to read it live, he objected to the censorship and walked out of the studio, leaving the BBC with an embarrassing 20 minutes of unfilled airtime. The "banned broadcast," as it became known in left-wing circles, was regarded by many liberals, who might not have been sympathetic to Ferrie's political position, as a prime example of the BBC's wish to control and constrain public speech. Even J.B. Priestley's wartime *Postscripts to the News*, which attracted an audience comprising one in three of Britain's adult population, met with government disapproval, leading Priestley to complain that the Corporation was controlled by the Ministry of Information which appeared to be, in turn, controlled by the War Cabinet. Nonetheless, a gradual movement in the direction of controversial discussion reflected an implicit acknowledgment within the BBC that not all broadcast voices could be rehearsed and edited.

A third task facing the early BBC was to move beyond the earnest solemnity of high-minded, often didactic commentary. Its mass audience was clearly interested in other aspects of everyday life from those that preoccupied the BBC Talks Department. The BBC responded to popular culture in a way that was to have far-reaching consequences. It established new, lighter-style programs, such as *In Town Tonight* (which remained a part of the BBC schedule from 1931 until 1960) which set out to reflect the lives of ordinary people. With a mix of vox pops, interviews with eccentric individuals, and features on the oddities of mundane culture, *In Town Tonight* offered the public a picture of itself, albeit one that too often depicted "ordinary people" as objects of amusement. In this way, the BBC created a problematic dichotomy between images of the public and accounts of public affairs. This was an inherently hierarchical division of audience labor, which relegated most people to the apparently apolitical world of everyday experience, while matters concerning institutional and wider social power inhabited a narrative form which anticipated a public capable of making intelligent civic judgments. The former were directed mainly towards women and the less educated; the latter towards the kind of people who thought they had a stake in the latest news. *In Town Tonight*, and later television shows such as *Candid Camera* (arguably the first reality TV show) and *Nationwide*, succeeded in capturing an image of the public as lively, witty, and diverse, but at the same time lacking its own historical agency; people to whom funny things happened rather than makers of their own destiny. Wilfred Pickles, whose show *Billy Welcome* took him into wartime factories to interview "ordinary" people, reflected in his memoirs on the patronizing nature of the format:

I hated the job. There were marching songs and sentimental melodies and I would interview those folks about their war jobs. There were personal endeavour stories in which a young mother told us about her own effort. "Looking after three children and still doing a grand job in the factory. Good lass," I would say, giving her a pat on the back. How I

loathed it, and how embarrassed I felt . . . It was rank propaganda under
a cloak of entertainment and it tormented me throughout the several
months that it ran.[15]

The BBC's drift towards communicative sociability was accelerated
by the political demands of World War II, which was being fought
(ostensibly, at least) for democracy. A new vocabulary of common
national identity and inclusive citizenship emerged, forcing the BBC to
recast its relationship with its listeners, who came to be seen as citizens,
not merely listening in, but engaged in multidimensional lifeworlds of
their own. BBC wartime programs, such as *My Day's Work*, *We Speak For
Ourselves*, *The World We Want*, and *Politics and the Ordinary Man*, sought
to reflect the diverse voices and experiences of real people. The highly
controversial introduction in 1941 of Wilfred Pickles as a newsreader,
with a broad Yorkshire accent, was symbolic of this attempt to create
an inclusive civic voice.

Despite these important stylistic adaptations, which made public service broadcasting sound and feel more like the audience it addressed,
this remained a space dedicated to cultural management rather than
autonomous expression. As Ouellette has suggested, in her insightful study
of early American public television, to be a good viewer-citizen "meant
accepting an aesthetic order governed by a higher authority. It required
access or acquiescence to communicative 'codes' rooted in the special-
ized habitus of legitimated opinion leaders."[16] As with all projects
intended to cultivate and maintain norms of national citizenship, this
model of the public sphere was defined by its limits. The industrial control of media production precluded untrammeled participation by all.
As with the bourgeois public sphere, a conflict between structures of
entrenched power and principles of unrestricted agency blighted the
democratic claims of public space.

Active Citizenship and the
Participatory Public Sphere

A third model of the public sphere, ascendant in the post-deferential culture of the post-World War Two era, conceives the space of the media
as one in which the public – or publics – can shape their own culture,

without state power or economic inequality constraining their capacity to act. Based on Dewey's conception of an intimate linkage between participation and reciprocity, whereby each person has to refer his own action in relation to that of others and to consider other's action as providing purpose and direction for one's own, the idea of the media as a space for active citizenship contrasts with the notion of mediation as authoritative dissemination.[17] At least four developments in the late twentieth century began to give credibility to the idea of a participatory public sphere.

The first was a growing sense that a new contract needed to be forged between authoritative institutions (governments, broadcasters, public services) and their users and supporters. In a socially mobile, post-deferential, increasingly democratizing society, neither the public nor the audience could any longer be taken for granted. Drawing on earlier radical counter-visions of media development, such as Brecht's (1936) claim that "Radio must be changed from a means of distribution to a means of communication. Radio would be the most wonderful means of communication imaginable in public life, a huge linked system – that is to say, it would be such if it were capable not only of transmitting but of receiving, of allowing the listener not only to hear but to speak, and did not isolate him [*sic*] but brought him into contact,"[18] commentators began to imagine a democratic role for broadcasting. The thread which connected these various radical positions was a rejection of rigid demarcations between media production and reception. Enzensberger, in his seminal 1970 essay, "Constituents of a theory of the media," declared that

> For the first time in history, the media are making possible mass parti-
> cipiation in a social and socialized productive process, the practical means
> of which are in the hands of the masses themselves . . . In its present
> form, equipment like television or film does not serve communication
> but prevents it . . . Electronic techniques recognize no contradiction in
> principle between transmitter and receiver.[19]

Raymond Williams, the most significant analyst and critic of media paternalism in the 1960s, argued that there were four available models of mass communication. Media could perform an authoritarian function, simply transmitting "the instructions, ideas, and attitudes of the ruling group." They could have a "paternal" character, which

Williams defined as "an authoritarian system with a conscience." Media could take a commercial form, claiming to reflect public demand as expressed through the asymmetrical power relationships of the market. Or they could perform a democratic role in which "all men [*sic*] have the right to 'transmit and the right to receive.' "[20] Groombridge, in his radical manifesto for television, argued that

> in addition to educating, informing and entertaining individuals, it should . . . (a) help the disparate segments of society to communicate with one another; and (b) foster the integrity and dynamism of democracy.[21]

Clarion calls such as these were reflected in the BBC's managerial rhetoric of the time, and internationally, in such projects as Education TV, and later the Public Broadcasting Service, in the United States, which President Johnson declared would make the nation appear like a facsimile of the old Greek marketplace, where political deliberations took place in public. Increased channel competition, a growing culture of grass-roots participation, and an emerging ethos of autonomous cultural production all contributed to a belief, sometimes couched in rather teleological terms, that an evolutionary transition from an elitist cultural order to "a multi-form, pluralistic, divergent society"[22] was taking place.

Secondly, as the concept of "empowerment" came to dominate policy discourse in a range of contexts – from the treatment of school students to global transitions to a post-colonial order – the impact of institutional arrangements upon civic culture was much debated. A range of conferences and reports responded to what seemed to be a growing public disenchantment with cultural centralism by calling for a more pluralistic and accessible media sphere. A seminal UNESCO report, published in 1980, entitled *Many Voices One World, Towards a New More Just and More Efficient World Information and Communication Order*, caught the mood of the times:

> in multifarious forms, individuals and groups are more and more participating directly in communication processes – with existing media, through official or institutionalised media, via alternative media – and finding new, effective outlets for creative expression . . . Its further development is vital for the future, as failure to keep pace with social needs and technological advances can only mean that man [*sic*] will be subjected to increasingly dehumanized and alienating experiences.[23]

The report went on to assert a "right to communicate" and claimed that

> Without a two-way flow between participants in the process, without
> the existence of multiple information sources permitting wider selection,
> without more opportunity for each individual to reach decisions based
> on a broad awareness of divergent facts and viewpoints, without
> increased participation by readers, viewers and listeners in the decision-
> making and programming activities of the media – true democratization
> will not become a reality.[24]

At stake here was a conception of media citizenship which sought to
transcend the binaric division between the production and the consumption of public knowledge. Underlying it was the belief that in a
democracy the public should be more than the addressee of messages
from above and afar. The radical implication of this position has
been most successfully embodied in the anti-hegemonic practices of
alternative media which have served to increase "the public's sense of
confidence in its power to engineer constructive change."[25] Uncom-
promising in their resistance to the controlled public sphere, alternative
media have opened up spaces of autonomous interaction in which
publics can represent themselves. But, despite Downing's plea that these
initiatives should not "be dismissed as just a curious little experiment
for revolutionary culture freaks,"[26] they have tended to reach only
small sections of the public. (See chapter 4 for further analysis.)

Thirdly, visions of a more participatory media culture were indir-
ectly strengthened as scholars abandoned the simplistic media-effects
models that had dominated communication studies since the 1920s.
A new generation of audience theorists regarded media audiences as
being active and selective in their search to satisfy their needs for
information and communicative relationships. Having both *motives* for
seeking information or entering into communication and *expectations*
about what they will gain from such activity, audience members select
particular sources and content. According to uses and gratifications
theory, different people use the same sources and content for quite
separate reasons and with contrasting expectations, and media use
results in a range of *gratifications* derived from these differentiated
combinations of needs, motives, and expectations. The notion of "the active
audience" has been broadly interpreted and widely debated by communication scholars, with many turning to ethnographic methods in

order to understand how media are consumed in everyday life. Few scholars now believe in a simplistic division between passive, inert audiences and active, self-directing publics. The public is best understood as an active audience which cannot express or witness itself except in mediated forms; while the audience can be understood as a putative public which not only listens in and watches media content, but makes its own sense of it, interacts with it, and, in some cases, reconfigures it for its own purposes. As audiences enter ever more active and inter-active roles, making their own sense of polysemic media texts and engaging with media content in ways that reconfigure it, they come to assume an identity that has more usually been attributed to the public. And as the public increasingly receives and sends its messages through mediated channels, from phone-ins to emails to reality television votes, it comes to look remarkably like an active audience. Manin's notion of an "audience democracy" is relevant here.[27]

Fourthly, new forms of media production emerged that challenged the claim of mainstream media to constitute the only effective model for public communication. One challenge came from community radio, which had emerged in the United States in the post-World War II era. The movement had two sources: the needs of ethnic minorities in urban conurbations to hear radio in their own languages (German, Italian, Polish, Yiddish, Russian) and the repressive political climate during the years of the Cold War which motivated activists to identify radio as a valuable weapon in the struggle to subvert the pro-war and anti-communist hysteria which seethed through the country. In the 1960s and 1970s, community radio appealed to proponents of counter-culture and expanded to various regions of the world, often with an explicit purpose of providing a more democratic space for public communica-tion. The participatory character of these media was based upon the rejection of notions of the mass audience passively receiving befriend-ing and edifying messages through the vertical flow of broadcast trans-mission. Community broadcasting is seen as a mass medium which is both participatory and controlled, albeit by activists located squarely in a locale and operating along democratic lines.

A second challenge to mainstream media forms came from cable television. A 1972 ruling by the US Federal Communications Com-mission (FCC) declared that cable operators had an obligation to provide access channels for educational, local government, and public use. This was seen by some enthusiasts as having the potential to empower a hitherto rather powerless polity, thereby restoring a sense of humanity to a society dehumanized by increasingly high levels of restrictive legislation which characterize much of the modern world. Experiments in community access to media technologies led to enthusiasm for new forms of public media not based upon the traditional flow of messages from elites to mass audiences. In Canada, Henaut and Klein's pioneering work with the *Challenge for Change* project gave communities access to video technology which enabled them to record their social concerns which were shown at public meetings and to government officials.[28] But such democratic experimentation was dampened before long by harsh economic realities: the deregulatory atmosphere within which cable television flourished was not ultimately conducive to civic imperatives and investment in viewer feedback declined, except for such services as tele-shopping and evangelical pay-to-pray schemes.

A third challenge came from experiments in "teledemocracy," which aimed (well before the emergence of the Internet) to test the potential of interactive communication systems that were based on the increasing convergence between broadband cable television, telecommunications, and computers. In 1972, Etzioni developed the MINERVA (Multiple Input Network for Evaluating Reactions, Votes and Attitudes) project, designed to enable "masses of citizens to have discussions with each other, and which will enable them to reach group decisions without leaving their homes or crowding into a giant hall."[29] The system involved telephone conferencing, radio, two-way cable TV, and satellites. In the 1980s, a number of "televote" experiments in Honolulu, Hawaii, and Southern California were conducted, in which random groups of citizens were contacted by telephone, invited to study a brochure containing policy information and varied opinions and then asked to vote on a policy question. With their promise of the possibility of direct democracy through instant polling of the population on any issue of the day, community media appeared to be challenging conventional approaches to both public broadcasting and democratic governance.

In all of these ways, belief in the feasibility of a public sphere based upon the principles of participation and reciprocity took root in the twentieth century. It gave rise to a forceful critique of the established media system for its failure to meet the norms of democracy that it professed to be serving. It led critics to question the capacity of media institutions to separate themselves from narrow economic interests, political influences, and elitist predilections; to focus upon the disadvantages of audiences and publics in their search for trustworthy information; and to explore policy strategies and options that might enhance the legitimacy of public voice. These themes are taken up in the next three chapters.

3

The Managed Public

The mediated public voice is managed in countless ways. It is edited, cut off in its prime, reduced to polling numbers, confined to banal soundbites, marginalized as background noise, rendered unofficial. From crowd scenes on the evening news to the ceaseless babble of callers to phone-ins, the voice of the public is characterized by indistinctiveness. Media professionals regularly invoke "the public interest" as a knee-jerk defense against criticisms of their seemingly insatiable appetite for prurience, sensationalism, celebrity-chasing, and numerous other misdeeds perpetrated in the name of giving the public what it wants, needs, and deserves. In this chapter, we argue that the media, and news media in particular, routinely decide what's in the best interest of the public, usually based on nothing more than musings at editorial team meetings and inklings about what typical members of the public are like and would expect from the mass media. Media professionals would say that they practice their craft within a tried and tested framework of values learnt in college and further consolidated on the job. These values tend to emphasize the importance of gatekeeping and filtering mechanisms intended to protect editorial content from both the ill-informed contributions and the unsophisticated demands of the mass public. The public's voice is far from being entirely absent from the contemporary media, but where it does appear it is highly managed, bounded all round by a journalistic lens which frames our/their words in particular ways.

Our aim in this chapter is to explore the ways in which the public's voice is managed in and through the news media. We begin by conceptualizing the sense in which the media's relationship with the public is conceived in spatial terms, with distinctly differing roles and expectations attributed to insiders and outsiders. We then consider three ways in which this spatial relationship is managed. Firstly, we consider the way in which certain voices are marginalized or excluded through the process of source selection for media stories. Secondly, we examine the ways in which the public are invited in to a range of media formats, such as letters to the editor, phone-ins and studio-based discussions, designed to involve members of the public, while keeping them firmly in their place. Thirdly, we explore the claims and limitations of media realism as formats of authentic public representation. It would be a mistake to read this chapter as evidence of a conspiracy by the mainstream media to silence the voice of the public. Many media professionals who are implicated in the strategies we discuss here would rightly object to such a simplistic account of their efforts to open up the media to the voices of "real people." They would say that they are simply doing their best to make good television or radio or to produce appealing newspapers or online content; that in a modern democratic society the media must let the public in to the media sphere; but that such inclusion must be managed if the quality of media output is to be sustained or improved. The critique set out in this chapter is not intended to challenge such operational judgments, but to question the conceptual foundations of long-standing assumptions about which voices most deserve to be heard and to report some empirical findings concerning current media representations of a range of public voices.

The Media as Sacred Space

Discussion of the media is replete with spatial metaphors which enable them to be imagined as constituting a physical entity occupying a center or series of centers. The studio is a classical example of such a center. The studio's function is to send out messages to an audience that is somewhere out there. Professional occupants of the studio are required to imagine the place of the distant audience: usually that place is the home, and typically the home revolves around the relationships of an imagined family. Viewers and listeners can only ever imagine the studio and the complex routines around which it is organized. Occasionally, members of the audience are invited into the studio – physically or virtually – but their entry is always consciously from the outside where they belong and their status can only ever be that of guests. The same is true when studio professionals descend upon real people's homes, thrusting their microphones and cameras into lives that they are used to addressing in a disembodied form. The media can only "go outside" on the basis of a reflexive understanding that it is beyond its own space. These acknowledgments and practices contribute to what we might call a media phenomenology, which organizes experience of the world around its own implicit and metaphorical map of power. The public, in the form of a mass audience, is put in its place, from which it can only escape by invitation, trespass, or total withdrawal. The public is distanced, while media organizations internalize and institutionalize the power of mass communication.

Spatial metaphors help to make sense of a fundamental change in the nature of social interaction, commonly associated with the rise of modernity. Premodern societies relied upon the physical transportation of symbolic forms in order to cross distances. Letters, for example, had to be written in one place and physically delivered to another by a vast postal service. With the emergence of telegraphy, messages that would once have had to take the form of letters could be communicated across distances without the need for physical transportation. As Thompson has shown, such "uncoupling of space and time" made possible for the first time communication based upon "despatialized simultaneity,"[1] an important consequence of which has been a change in the ways that people experience time and space. Broadcasting, in particular, has generated feelings of liveness which leave audiences believing that they are indeed witnessing events as they happen, even though they might be thousands of miles away. Giddens refers to a "stretching" of social relations, so that, even though our direct experience is of the local and immediate, it is influenced and reconfigured by all kinds of indirect and mediated experiences, not least of which are those we read about in the press or see on television.[2] Power acts increasingly across distances, reshaping not only the rules of everyday life, but the very experience of being alive. The media organizations which facilitate this reordering of time, space, and experience assume an almost sacred status, not simply producing publications or programs which the public receives and try to make sense of, but producing schedules, norms, skills, tones, taboos, and worldviews which contribute to the public's sense of self-identity, routine, and security. In short, the media do not merely transmit messages, they contribute significantly to shaping the social, ethical, and affective conditions of message reception. While the public is occasionally allowed in to the former aspect of the media's role – the transmission of messages – it is hardly ever invited to participate in the ultimately more influential task of determining how social relations can be stretched by investing them with meaning and seductive value. We might summarize this complex argument by saying that, whereas the public is sometimes, and under strict conditions, allowed on to the media, the terms of mediation remain off limits to the public. The management of sensitive spatial relationships between national and global events and the public remain under the control of a small range of media institutions not well known for their accountability.

Thinking of the media as a space has important implications for the conceptual mapping of public and private relationships. The paradox of the mass media is that content is produced for public consumption, but mainly received within private spaces. Frustratingly for them media institutions can control every aspect of production, but have few ways of managing reception. Indeed, as Ang has observed, "Contrary to other social institutions such as the school or the family, television (as well as all other mass media) does not have the means to coerce people into becoming members of its audience."[3] Unable to make people watch or receive intended messages, the media must constantly operate with an awareness of the potential gap between production objectives and consumption experience. This space is potentially empowering for the public which, by switching off or over to other channels, can punish deceptive, condescending, dull, or opaque content producers. It is in this *space between* the public and the media that meanings are offered, negotiated, or discarded; claims to popularity are put to the test; representations are played out; and the incessant ambiguities of mediation are most vividly experienced.

On those occasions when the doors of the media are opened wide enough for the public to enter – in studio discussions, phone-ins, interactive votes, or letters to the editor – much care is taken to create an aura of intimacy. The daytime talk show might be transmitted into millions of households, but the illusion of the homely set design is that the guest have just popped in to pull up an armchair next to Oprah or Rikki or Vanessa. The phone-in might be seeking to reach a vast, dispersed audience – the elderly in their homes; taxi drivers on the road; the background babble in garages and workshops – but the caller must be persuaded that she is on the line to the host, engaged in a kind of conversation that links two, not two hundred thousand, people. The letter-writer to the local newspaper is required to affect the illusion of addressing his remarks to the ever-interested editor, even though the real reason for writing is to obtain a few published lines that will be read by an unknown public. The simulation of intimate, sociable space serves a prosthetic function, concealing the institutional impersonality of attempts to address a mass audience by pretending that the inner space of media production is but an extension of the privately experienced realities of the countless spectators "out there." To make sense of this process, we need to consider specific ways in which this relationship between spaces of lived and mediated experience are managed.

Cutting the Public Out – the Problem of Source Selection

The breadth and diversity of public voice is narrowed through source selection. Most mainstream media professionals tend to converge around a broadly conservative set of criteria relating to source credibility which results in the privileging of official rather than dissident voices, traditional views over the radical, and men's voices over those of women. Who is invited to give their accounts of reality and speak as commentators on and in the news says crucially important things about whose voices have legitimacy and social status. If news reports are based on the inclusion of *these* voices on *those* topics, then the power of media professionals to include (or exclude) all those other voices and topics is important. A cursory glance at any newspaper demonstrates that a majority of mainstream news stories, other than editorials, round-ups and opinion pieces, regularly feature either a source's actual words or else a paraphrase of something said. The use of sources is thus an extremely important part of the construction and orientation of a story. The ways in which knowledge is constructed and the sources used privilege those social actors who meet journalistic criteria of credibility and who fit within a normative framework which renders important those voices which know how to play the game. Recent changes in media production practices – the 24/7 news cycle, with fewer staff doing more jobs, serving ever-more channels and outlets – means that organizational pressures to get copy ready quickly encourages journalists to use familiar and non-controversial sources, falling back on individuals whose place in the economic and/or political hierarchy provides instant status.

Bias in source selection usually plays out to the considerable detriment of groups that are in conflict with elites, such as campaign activists. There is a reluctance on the part of most sections of the news media to cover protest politics in anything other than negative terms, with some journalists even conflating "protest" with "terrorism."[4] In one study of news stories, researchers found that a mere 2 percent of items made any reference to citizen action.[5] If we accept the existence of even the most benign form of agenda-setting on the part of the press, then *who* is allowed to speak in the news is just as important as *which* stories are selected for inclusion. Who speaks matters because access to the media is access to persuasive influence. Even in so-called non-political stories, the people chosen to comment on, say, a new building development or the closure of a hospital or the incidence of distraction burglaries, help to shape how issues are considered and viewed, and contribute to a hegemonic understanding of whose views are important. By obscuring selection and perspective, the fiction of impartiality and balance enables media professionals to appear as mere conveyors of others' views, while actually promoting a particular line by the choice of speakers and quotes. In the few studies of news sources which have been undertaken, findings have tended to show that the principal contributors are white male elites, with "ordinary" citizens, women, and members of ethnic minorities, being far less frequently identified.[6] The persistent use of conventional, high-status sources can be understood as a journalistic norm. Even when more diverse views *are* reported, such coverage tends to be constrained within the boundaries of institutional tolerance. It is not just the reporting of a story which matters, but the choice of source influences both its shape and its orientation, casually but irrevocably promoting a particular perspective which goes unchallenged. Even during election campaigns, which are the times when the public's voice is most frequently sought by journalists, most news stories are still overwhelmingly populated by the party leaders. Similarly, in almost every study which specifically looks at gender salience in source selection, men are *always* more frequently heard, quoted, and reported than women.

The hierarchy of news values identified more than 25 years ago[7] which gave value to some voices and not others, shows no sign of disappearing in the twenty-first century. Citizens are simply not represented in the media on equal terms with government spokespeople. And, as the case study below shows, women are rarely represented on equal terms with men.

News Sources and the Local Press: Three Local Newspapers in Middle England

The study on which this case is based sought to answer two specific questions: first, are women and men differently represented as (local) newspaper sources, in gross volume terms, in status terms, and by story topic; and secondly, what is the balance between "elite" sources and those of the general public.[8] Three newspapers were sampled – the *Birmingham Post*, the *Coventry Evening Telegraph* and the *Leicester Mercury* – and monitored over a ten-week period, one day each week, making a total of ten weekdays over the period. The three newspapers were chosen mostly as a convenience sample but also because they share a broad regional geographic boundary, serve broadly similar communities, and have similar circulations in relation to population size.

A total of 30 newspapers were thus monitored (three newspapers each day over ten monitoring days) and a total of 538 articles were analyzed and 925 individual sources coded. What we found was that although members of the public were better represented as sources in this sample of news stories than has been demonstrated elsewhere, they still only comprised less than a quarter of *all* sources, with far more preference given to "elite" voices such as those from the business world (usually managers of businesses), professional occupations such as doctors, lawyers, and teachers, together with councillors and local government workers. Human interest stories attracted the largest volume of sources and, unsurprisingly, were also the story type in which members of the public were most likely to be asked their opinion or to be quoted. Women were three times more likely to be asked to speak as members of the public than men and they had a significant presence as education workers and as spokespeople for the charitable and voluntary sector, areas of work which are typically undertaken by women. By contrast, men were twice as likely as women to be asked to speak as business people, three times more likely to speak as local councillors, and nearly three times as likely to speak as police officers.

The absolute number of sources was still heavily biased towards men so that even in the category of "human interest" which appeared to favor women, the actual numbers of women and men quoted in these 122 stories were 75 and 138 respectively. In only two categories (local celebrity and sex-discrimination) did absolute numbers of women sources exceed men. In only one category (pets/animals) did women and men achieve parity but every-where else, women were outnumbered by a ratio of at least 1 : 2, and often an even higher ratio than this. It is only as "members of the public" where the absolute numbers of women and men sourced across all story types are almost identical (112 and 111 respectively). What the findings from this, admittedly modest, study show is that who speaks in the news and who writes the news is alarmingly similar in the local press as in the nationals. This is not just in terms of the dominance of elite voices over "the public," of men's voices over those of women, of white voices over black, but also in terms of who writes the news, the beats which are awarded to journalists (i.e. women do culture and home, men do politics and the economy, again) and the types of story which make it into print.

Letting the Public In: From Letters to the Editor to Audience Participation

Although the mass media have traditionally relied upon a few-to-many flow of communication, there have always been moments of feedback when the audience has a chance to respond to what is being directed at them. Although media interactivity is most commonly associated with computer-mediated communication, it did not originate with the possibility for digital feedback. Audiences have always had a range of ways of responding and contributing to media texts. Even reading a newspaper involves elementary forms of interactivity insofar as readers decide what to read, in what order to do so, and whether to put pen to paper and submit a letter for publication commenting on what has been read. Media interactivity, via letters to the editor, calls to phone-ins, participation in a vocal studio audience, or sending a message to a media website, provides an opportunity for the public to make its presence felt in a mediated context by transcending the spatial barriers which usually characterize the producer–audience relationship.

Interactive participation is enriched when the space between encountering content and registering a response diminishes. For example, writing a letter to a newspaper expressing opposition to a politician's remarks involves a different spatial and historical relationship from calling a phone-in program while a politician is on the air to complain about what she is saying. The extent to which interactivity can be said to occur is determined by the objective and perceived capacities of audiences to respond meaningfully to media content. Bucy has argued that mediated interaction should be regarded as a subjective experience; that some interactive encounters *feel* more like an unmediated relationship than others.[9] Democratic outcomes are most likely to arise from situations in which technical and cultural opportunities for interactivity result in perceived experiences of authentic interaction. With a view to exploring the strengths and weaknesses of these potentially democratizing prospects, we shall consider three participatory formats: letters to the editor, radio phone-in programs and audience-based studio discussions.

Dear editor . . .

Since the rise of the mass franchise and widespread adult literacy in the late nineteenth century, the media have created small but important openings for public feedback and open expression. "Letters to the editor" are the earliest form of such cracks in the media edifice, conspicuously embracing and encouraging the public's right to offer comment on the events of the day, as well as the fairness and accuracy of press coverage. Through the letters column, members of the public have an opportunity to contribute to the discursive atmosphere surrounding particular events or policies. "Letters to the editor," for all the criticism that they are written by people who have too much time on their hands or whose opinions fall into the extreme ends of the public spectrum, contribute to a public sphere insofar as they enable citizens to discuss issues that will reach a wider audience. Often, especially in the case of local newspapers, letters from the public facilitate a rudimentary dialogue, opening up fractures within and between publics, and allowing disagreements to be rehearsed – and occasionally even settled – through a process of letters and responses over a series of weeks.

Speculation about the representativeness of opinions expressed in "letters to the editor" is of limited value because there is a dual process of mediation taking place: firstly, writers are self-selecting and second, letters selected for publication are filtered and often abridged. Even if letter-writers are not truly representative of the wider public, published letters still comprise a fascinating set of texts, precisely because they tend to be written from the experiential perspective of ordinary people rather than by journalists or politicians. But to what extent do letters which are antithetical to the primary political orientation of a newspaper, or even directly critical of the editorial policy, still get published? Most readers accept that some kind of selection and editing of letters must take place and letters will often be abridged, but how risky is it to publish a radical or critical letter in the mainstream press? Since newspapers are in the business of making money, and since being conspicuously controversial can sell newspapers, it is sometimes the case that inflammatory letters will be chosen rather than more moderate ones. But, generally speaking, empirical studies suggest that by far the majority of published letters are broadly conformist to the newspaper's agenda and supportive of the status quo will be in the majority.

Letterboxes and Gatekeepers

In Karin Wahl-Jorgensen's work with letters' editors at several newspapers in the San Francisco Bay area in the late 1990s, she sets out a tripartite model of writer motivation which she names as dialogist, activist, and exhibitionist and explores the extent to which the perceived motivation to write influences the decision to publish.[10] She explored the decision-making process for letter selection, probing editors to identify the kinds of letters they liked and disliked. What emerged from her research was the identification of two specific editor preferences which together work to frame very narrowly the public's discourse. The preferences were, firstly, for the individual (Joanne Public) over the collective (activist), and second, for the emotional over the rational. Wahl-Jorgensen argues that both rational (dialogic) and activist letter-writers are thus passed over in favor of the exhibitionist because of editors' preference for the highly charged and emotional letter, full of anecdote and personalized account. The letters' page is denied its potential to function as part of a genuinely public sphere because the gate-keepers of this particular space are suspicious of the "hidden agendas" of activist letter-writers; one editor in Wahl-Jorgensen's study described such letters as dishonestly concealing the real point, "in a bunch of mumbo jumbo." Thus the filtering lens of journalistic thrill-seeking and distaste for rational and challenging argument undermines the news industry claims to speak on "our" behalf by imposing their own values of sensation over any alleged responsibility to inform the public through the provision of balanced content.

Letter-writers put themselves in a highly competitive environment where the rules of the game are not at all apparent. Filtering mechanisms are always in play, but the principles and rules of such mechanisms usually remain implicit and opaque, leaving letter-writers guessing as to what might constitute acceptable material and why some contributions are rejected without appeal. The hidden hand of the editorial decision moves in mysterious ways. In one of the very few sustained studies of editorial decision-making in relation to publication of readers' letters, it was suggested that editors prefer letters which introduce new ideas into particular policy debates, thus constituting an important feedback loop from the public to the media and perhaps also to the politicians.[11] But, although this is laudable and very much in keeping with the idea of media in the public interest, what remains hidden in such high-minded editorial rhetoric are the criteria whereby one letter is included and another is rejected. As other studies show, there is considerable dissonance between journalistic rhetoric and how the editing pen is actually wielded, with newsroom staff often holding rather ungenerous attitudes towards the letter-writing public including a view that they are mostly mad.[12]

The extent to which public letter-writers can influence policy is unclear. While readers of newspapers who also write in to them cannot necessarily be regarded as representing the views of readers in general, they do indicate the presence of engaged citizens with something to say, however extreme that might sometimes be. By articulating their views, they are enabling a more thoughtful public to better understand the nuances of particular issues and the range of (often unreported) positions that can be adopted towards them. In this sense, citizens' desire to influence policy through personal advocacy in newspaper letters' columns provides evidence of an enduring form of active citizenship, even if its political efficacy is unclear.

Calling in

Radio phone-ins – talk shows in which listeners can call in by telephone and express their views on air – might be regarded as a technologically developed version of letters to the editor. They provide a faster form of interactive communication, creating scope for members of the audience to engage directly with mediated content.

Most studies of phone-ins as spaces for public political expression have concentrated upon the North American format that became popular in the 1980s in which mainly (but not exclusively) conservative hosts have sought to appeal to the illiberal prejudices of a core audience. Understandably, far from constituting anything resembling a public sphere, these shows have been regarded as vehicles for group herding and uncivil debate. Some suggest that phone-ins in which reasonable debate has become argumentation for its own sake and order has become chaos[13] are symptomatic of a "dumbing down" of politics, reducing public debate to the lowest levels of populist entertainment.

But there are other traditions of interactive radio discussion which amount to more than mere public noise. In the depression of the 1930s, the radio show *Vox Pop* began broadcasting the voices of the public as a specific response to the desire to give some power to the people.

Throughout the course of its 16-year run, its protean and ambivalent uses of the voice of the people also exemplified the populism that characterized the emerging mass-mediated public sphere of the 1930s and 1940s. With such precedents in terms of intent, is it possible to see in some contemporary radio phone-in shows an authentic engagement of the public with the political process, with raw voices and excited opinions demonstrating something real rather than the bluff/double-bluff which routinely takes place between professional interviewers and the political elite?

During the 2001 UK general election, we conducted research on *Election Call*, the BBC Radio 4 daily political phone-in. *Election Call* is a series which has been broadcast before British general elections since 1974. In previous series each program ran for one hour, but in 2001 broadcast time was cut to 45 minutes, with an additional 15-minute webcast added on to the end, available only via the Internet. In 1997 the series was simulcast on the TV channel BBC1, Radio 4 and online via BBC Online. In 2001 the series remained on Radio 4 and online, but was shifted to BBC2, away from a wider TV audience, as this is regarded as the BBC's more highbrow channel. The series was presented by Peter Sissons (as in 1997) and featured one guest politician each weekday from May 21, to June 6, except for one day when the two leaders of the Scottish National Party (SNP) and Plaid Cymru (the Welsh nationalist party) appeared together. The Labour and Conservative Parties had four politicians each as program guests; the Liberal Democrats had three, on the grounds that Labour and Conservative are regarded as the major players. The public was invited to call a telephone number and put their points to the politicians.

Our research, which we cannot summarize in full here, involved the following process:

- daily attendance at the *Election Call* studio by at least two members of the research team;
- daily counts of all call slips, to determine number of callers wanting to go on air and number of calls aired;
- analysis of all call slips, to determine age and gender of all callers and whether their intended topics conformed to the set of "target" topics outlined by the producer that morning;
- stopwatch time analysis of all comments made throughout the series, with time graphs produced for each program;

- analysis of a national poll of *Election Call* viewers and listeners, as well as examination of comments submitted by respondents;
- follow-up calls to 80 callers: 68 whose calls were aired on the program and 12 whose calls were not selected;
- regular attendance by one researcher before and during the production of the webcast;
- interviews with members of the production team.

Our aim here is to describe who the callers were, the extent to which they set their own agenda and how far they regarded their brief access to the media – and to senior politicians – as an authentically democratic opportunity.

There are two images of the typical phone-in caller. On the one hand, there exists a disparaging image of phone-in callers as opinionated bores, endlessly recycling misinformation and prejudice. It is a crude image, drawn more often than not from the early days of British local radio and the US "dittoheads" who populate the ubiquitous shock jock shows. On the other hand, there is an image of phone in callers as a "public voice," informal representatives of the silent majority. Which of these images is more correct? Our analysis can only shed light on callers to *Election Call*, but it certainly does provide us with a clear picture of the representativeness of this group.

In all, 2,760 calls – an average of 230 per day – were answered by telephonists over the 12-day period of the series and one call slip was filled in for each of these. Some callers to the program will have failed to get through to the switchboard, but our estimation, on the basis of the general lack of pressure upon telephonists to answer calls, was that these would not constitute a significant addition to the number whose calls were taken.

Who did the 2,760 calls come from? On the basis of our analysis of the information provided on all call slips, we can report that callers were overwhelmingly male and over 45 years old; 70 percent of callers were male and 30 percent of calls came from women. There was no evidence of women guest politicians receiving more (or fewer) calls from women. Twenty-five percent of callers were over 65 years old. Approximately 15 percent of the UK population is aged over 65, so the calls received from this group were significantly disproportionate. We would attribute this to the timing of the program (9 a.m.), when other potential callers are at work, and the generally higher interest in politics amongst the 65+ age group. A mere 6 percent of callers were under 25 years old.

Out of this pool of 2,760 calls, 139 were used on air: on average, 11 calls per day. The fate of most callers is to reach no further in the selection process than the telephonists who answer their call. When considering the small percentage of successful callers who made it on to the air, we can see the extent to which the producers reinforced or redressed demographic imbalances. In the case of gender, the balance of used calls precisely (though undoubtedly unintentionally) replicated the 70 : 30 male : female balance of overall calls to the program. Despite claims to be seeking more calls from women, the producers did nothing to upset the considerable imbalance between calls taken from men and women.

In the case of age, a much more energetic production agenda can be discerned. Although 25 percent of all calls received came from over-65s, only 18 percent were put on air. Conversely, while only 6 percent of calls received came from under-25s, 12 percent of calls put on air came from this age group. Of course, we are not suggesting that the *Election Call* producers were filtering used calls on the basis of callers' age, but there was a clear attempt being made to emphasize the voice of youth. On several occasions researchers observed telephonists calling out that they had managed to find a young caller and these were treated at the next production stage as rare and precious commodities. Younger callers were given greater freedom to veer away from the established election agenda onto issues that were relevant to their experience. On the contrary, many older callers wanted to raise issues concerning long-term care or pensions and these tended to be crowded out during the selection process.

To what extent were the callers who did manage to make it on to the air able to make themselves heard? Overall, 54.8 percent of all program time was taken by politicians talking – an average of 23 minutes and 58 seconds per program. Callers occupied 30.9 percent of overall time – an average, 13 minutes and 31 seconds per program. The presenter took up 10.3 percent of the time – on average, 4 minutes and 42 seconds per program. (This compares with 1997 when politicians spoke for 60 percent of overall time, callers for 27 percent of the time, and the presenter for 12 percent of the time. So, there has been a gradual movement away from loquacious politicians towards more talkative callers, with Peter Sissons playing a far less conspicuous role than did Robin Day in the 1979 *Election Call* series when he spoke for 31.3 percent of overall program time.)

So, some members of the audience were able to speak in ways that would not have been possible in most political programs, but still they were allowed less time to raise questions and develop arguments than was afforded to the guest professional politicians. To what extent, however, were callers able to expand or re-order the election agenda set by the politicians and broadcasters? The existence of media agendas is well known and frequently analyzed. The production of political broadcasts is highly dependent upon themes and issues brought to prominence through systemic relationships between the main political parties, the press, and broadcasters. It would be surprising if *Election Call*, which is produced by BBC news and politics professionals, did not reflect the agenda priorities of the wider news media. The key question here is whether the program's interactive format merely allowed the public to voice its own comments on a publicly determined agenda or whether the calling public was enabled to establish elements of its own agenda.

In order to go beyond speculation to analysis, it was necessary to construct a model of each day's media agenda. This was made relatively simple for us by the producers' daily briefing to the telephonists in which the main issues of the agenda were outlined. The producers were concerned to stress that their agenda was not the only one of interest and that they were eager for telephonists to be open to new and different issues raised by callers. But the fact that a daily outline of key issues was communicated to the telephonists can be reasonably regarded as a media agenda. Topics on this agenda were noted down each day and referred to in our research as MA. It was then necessary to analyze all call slips each day and note down the topics being raised by callers. We called these CA. To what extent did CA equal MA? Were callers raising MA topics more, less, or equally likely to appear on air than non-MA callers?

The results suggested a strong bias in favor of calls relating to the media agenda, as defined each morning by the producers. Of the 2,760 call slips analyzed, 21 percent could be classified as MA; 79 percent were non-MA call topics. Of the 139 calls that were taken on air, having gone through the producers' selection process, 39 percent were MA topics and only 61 percent were non-MA. This was not a partisan bias, but a clear tendency to use calls conforming to the producers' issue priorities and to reject calls that were inconsistent with the established agenda. In defense, the producers could reasonably argue that, even with the selection bias that we have uncovered, most calls to the program were non-MA ones. They could also argue that callers to the program do not constitute a representative sample of the population (as we have ourselves demonstrated above) and that MA topics are more likely to reflect the interests of viewers and listeners than would rejected non-MA ones. They may well be right about this, particularly as several of the non-MA topics related to policies of special interest to the over-65s, who were disproportionately represented as callers. But in that case the program producers should make it clear that *Election Call* is less a voice of callers than an attempt to reflect the voices of viewers and listeners – and in *that* case they would have even more of an incentive to seek to redress the unbalanced demographic profile of callers.

Finally, how did the callers perceive their experience of phone-in interactivity? Were they participating in what they perceived to be a authentically democratic event or did they think they were being used? As part of our research, we contacted by telephone each day half the successful callers (three women and three men), our selection being based on the variety of their topics and the political skew of the questions. The participants in our study certainly believed that they contributed to a meaningful dialogue through their participation in the program and also said that they were not just talking for themselves but also representing the views of "the public." If they were not exactly representing the so-called "ordinary" person in the street, then they were at least being representative of the public at large in terms of reflecting some significant political concerns. Motivations to call in were numerous but most popular were: desire to engage with a politician; anger over personal experience of bad service/treatment; and long-standing disquiet about a particular policy. Obviously, of crucial importance in a phone-in program which purports to enable dialogue between the public and the politicians, is the extent to which callers feel that they (and their question) have been treated seriously. When asked, fewer than half our respondents gave an unequivocal "yes" to this question, a quarter said that the politician *had* answered the question but only superficially or with some kind of spin, and just under one-third gave an unequivocal "no" or said they had been "fobbed off." Despite the relatively negative comments and criticism expressed by our callers towards the politicians, almost all our sample felt that participating in *Election Call* itself had been a worthwhile experience.

When we asked callers if they believe the program contributes to the democratic process in terms of the wider polity, there was a resounding "yes" from most of our sample, although men were significantly more positive than women whose caution related to the potential of the program really to provoke a change in attitudes amongst both politicians and the electorate at large. Part of that caution was a concern with *who* is actually listening, given that the show is broadcast in the early morning when many people are at work or taking children to school. Callers commented on their desire to hold politicians to account, to make them listen, and then, hopefully, to act. Above all, they welcomed the opportunity to put an unrehearsed question to a politician, to counter what appeared to many to be the most tightly managed election campaign they had ever witnessed. Whilst callers consciously acknowledged that politicians were unlikely to change their minds and policies as a consequence of their own critical intervention, they were much more optimistic about the program's awareness-raising potential amongst the listeners whose views *could* perhaps be influenced. As one caller we interviewed put it,

> I think that a lot of ordinary people feel frustrated. I mean there's been a lot of people that have said in the election campaign that both Blair and Hague [the leaders respectively of the Labour and Conservative Parties at the time] haven't stopped to speak to ordinary people, they've just had photo calls and the supporters and ordinary people can't stop to talk to them. I think that *Election Call* gives ordinary people – like however weird their questions are – the right to ask a question and I think that's very important.

The studio audience speaks

The two previous participatory formats we have looked at involve the use of technologies (post and telephony) to transcend traditional spaces that separate media audiences from broadcast content. The third example is rather different: here we are looking at ways in which media producers have used studio audiences to act as proxy voices for the wider public. In audience-participation shows, ranging from daytime confessional TV, such as *Oprah*, to political debates, such as BBC's *Question Time*, members of the public are invited to tell their stories, question experts, and arrive at collective moral judgments. Audience-participation shows have three defining features: firstly, they focus upon single social issues which are explored in personal terms; secondly, they are structured around the moral authority of hosts and experts whose role is to translate between official and lay knowledge; and thirdly, the studio-based audience is expected to participate actively, through both individual testimony and collective reactions.

The implicit rationale for the presence of members of the public on audience-participation shows is not that they have any special qualifications or fame, but precisely the opposite.

Some media theorists have argued that audience-participation formats create a space in which a mediated public sphere can emerge. For example, Livingstone and Lunt argue that audience discussion programs "offer an informal, unofficial, but nonetheless large-scale, institutionally managed forum for public debate."[14] Carpignano et al. are also optimistic about the democratic potential of audience-participation shows insofar as they place members of the public "literally on center stage" and entertain a more "therapeutic" approach to public reasoning, based upon experiential testimony rather than ideological rhetoric.[15] Indeed, there are good reasons for seeing audience-participation formats as possessing some of the characteristics of a public sphere: they are accessible by a broad audience which is not selected on the basis of status, qualification, or ability to pay; they discuss issues of common interest in vernacular terms, in which the political is frequently personalized and the personal politicized; they require experts to account for their beliefs and judgments before a lay, non-deferential public; and they are less likely to be male-dominated than many other public-deliberation fora.

While audience-participation formats certainly do provide more exposure to voices, experiences, and perspectives that were hitherto neglected or described in the third person, that in itself is not enough to demonstrate that they constitute, or even contribute to, the formation of a democratic public sphere. Audience-participation formats fall short of even the most basic norms of democracy in three particular ways. Firstly, these are highly managed media spaces in which participators are only allowed to enter and speak if they fit in with the format protocols of the producers. Murdock's observation that traditional, paternalistic broadcasters have sought "to foster 'ordinary people's' participation and inclusiveness within the body politic by excluding them from its own process of production"[16] points to the contradiction inherent in managed participatory formats. Even in the most apparently open studio discussion, members of the public are constrained in their behavior by expectations that have been explicitly or tacitly conveyed to them, as well as by forms of technical control that are monopolized, without any accountability, by the producers. For example, questioners on the BBC *Question Time* program know that the producers expect them to speak in the form of questions rather than statements; that their contributions should not exceed a matter of seconds rather than minutes; that they are likely to be cut off mid-flow if they attempt to offer historical analysis; that they are not supposed to talk among themselves; and that they are not entitled to offer views about the program format – for example, when to move on to a new question or whether to demand that one of the guest politicians stop prevaricating and answer the question. If audience participants fail to understand or abide by these tacit rules of expectation, the producers are free to intervene technologically: denying them access to a microphone; refusing to let them be seen on screen; or editing them out of a recorded discussion. In a democratic public sphere, one would expect these rules of debate to be agreed in advance and for there to be opportunities for those accused of rule-breaking to appeal against unwise or unjust decisions. In audience-participation programs, neither the rights nor the responsibilities of participants are transparent – and producers are quite free to move between benign tolerance of public expression and manipulative disregard for what the public really want to say.

A second objection to regarding audience-participation formats as spaces in which a democratic public sphere would be likely to emerge is the tendency of producers to present the public as a singular, univocal body, which can be represented either by the collective moral utterances of a recruited crowd or the predictable contributions of a "scientifically" assembled replica of public opinion. An audience-participation program which took place during the 1997 UK general election campaign provides an interesting case study of the consequences of seeking to construct a representative public.

Defining the Public

The *ITV 500* program, produced by Granada TV, originated as a format in the February 1974 UK general election. Five hundred voters from key marginal constituencies were assembled in a studio and invited to interrogate the leaders of the three major parties. As there is no tradition of televized leaders' debates in the UK, this opportunity to question party leaders consecutively was one of the major television moments during the 1997 election campaign. All three party leaders were invited to appear on the program, but Conservative Prime Minister, John Major, failed to attend and was represented by his deputy, Michael Heseltine. No sooner had the program commenced and the presenter, Sue Lawley, announced that Major would not be present than the audience began to heckle its first interviewee, Heseltine, complaining that Major had been too frightened to face them. Heseltine responded with vigor, explaining that Major was not there because he was bravely undertaking a secretly arranged visit to Northern Ireland. There then followed the first official question to Heseltine from an audience member who urged the politician to "stop conning us." Heseltine's response was interrupted several times by both further questions and derisive laughter. The presenter joined in a couple of times to urge the audience to allow the politician to have his say. At this point, Heseltine questioned the structure of the program in a way that raises interesting questions about the democratic claims of audience-participation political debates:

> HESELTINE: Let us not have any illusions. This audience is carefully selected to represent the political parties. And that's what it should be. So that means that on any normal statistics about two-thirds of this audience wants a Liberal or Labour candidate to win. So they will cheer anything that supports that side of the argument. The idea that this is a representative audience . . .
>
> LAWLEY: It is . . .
>
> HESELTINE: . . . who have got detached views . . .
>
> LAWLEY: . . . it is a cross-representative audience . . .
>
> HESELTINE: Exactly. That's what I'm saying.
>
> LAWLEY: It is a perfectly . . .

HESELTINE: It is an audience which is bound to give an anti-government slant. So I hope everybody at home will understand that.

LAWLEY: No, no, no, no, no . . .

AUDIENCE: (Noises of opposition)

HESELTINE: Of course it is. Of course it is. Of course it is.

LAWLEY: It is a scientifically selected audience of marginal constituents.

HESELTINE: It is a scientifically selected audience to give a representation of the present political system in this country which would mean that the government cannot have a majority in an audience of this sort. That's all I'm saying.

LAWLEY: Well, we've taken into consideration socioeconomic factors and all the rest. I think you should be getting as fair a hearing as scientifically you deserve. Let me have that lady there . . .

Heseltine's understandable concern here was that the viewing public would be influenced by the expressed bias of the studio audience which was designed to reflect the politically committed public. His rhetorical appeal to the public at home, as opposed to the public with him in the studio, constituted an attempt to override the program producers' claim that they had managed to construct a microcosm of the public sphere. This can be seen as a politically strategic illustration of what Scannell has called the "doubling of place": "Public events now occur, simultaneously, in two different places: the place of the event itself and that in which it is watched and heard."[17] In this instance, the politician adopted a strategy intended to win support from viewers "at home" rather than the studio audience whose viewing (and views) they are witnessing.

A third cause for doubt about the democratic potential of audience-participation formats concerns their relationship to political outcomes. Being free to air grievances or attribute responsibility for social ills are necessary, but not sufficient elements of a democratic public sphere. Public testimony and group therapy may well prepare the ground for social action, while at the same time failing to provide the public – either in the studio or watching on television – with opportunities to act upon their discussion in politically consequential ways. Similarly, Carpignano et al. argue that talk shows are "not cognitive but therapeutic"; that they provide "not a balance of viewpoints but a serial association of testimonials."[18] Such accounts explain the participatory function of audience-discussion formats in terms of collective therapy and system legitimacy, but these in themselves need not lead to democratic effects. Indeed, it is a mistake to speak about participation and democracy as if they were synonymous terms, for some participatory practices are embedded within quite undemocratic structures and are bound to lead to outcomes that ignore or diminish public experience.

The key question for proponents of participatory media, in all or any of its forms, is whether these formats do, or could in the future, have democratic political consequences. There are at least some grounds for thinking that they do and could. Firstly, there is some evidence to suggest that remote (rather than studio-based) audiences do feel represented by the voices of "ordinary people" they encounter through the media. As part of our *Election Call* study, we conducted a survey in which 3,555 members of the national BBC viewers' and listeners' panel were asked their views about these political phone-ins. Of the 4 percent of panel members who had heard the program on BBC Radio 4 and the 1 percent who had watched it on BBC2, 69 percent stated that "*Election Call* provided a real democratic voice for the people," 62 percent said that "The callers as a whole asked the type of questions I would want to ask" and one in four said that it "raised new issues for discussion with friends and family." These findings suggest that the program performed more than a therapeutic or legitimizing function; that, in terms of parasocial interaction, callers were performing a proxy role for the wider public, and listeners and viewers were pursuing the discussion beyond the context of reception. Indeed, some recent media scholarship has focused on the double articulation of broadcast communication, exploring the ways in which broadcast "talk is received in the context of the home." This involves interrogating "*how* the relationship between broadcasters and their audiences is accomplished through discursive (social) interaction."[19] In her study of how viewers of daytime television talk shows talked about what they were watching in the course of viewing, Wood found rich evidence of what she calls a "mediated conversational floor" in which viewers invested their own comments within the televized discussion, by, for example, addressing remarks to on-screen discussants, completing their sentences for them, stating their own opinions, or referring to their own experiences in empathy with on-screen speakers.[20] We cannot be sure how extensive such dislocated, parasocial participation might be, but it is at least a possibility that audien-ceparticipation formats might have discrete mobilizing and confidence-building effects that are hard to identify.

Secondly, audience-participation formats can sometimes serve to expose issues which might otherwise fail to achieve prominence within the elite-driven news agenda. By referring to their own experiences, or appearing to confront political rhetoric with everyday common sense, members of the public can deliver far more wounding attacks upon politicians and their policies than can professional journalists, who are perceived as playing by the same rules as politicians.

The Day Margaret Thatcher Met Her Match

One example of a member of the public holding a political leader to account in a way that was more forceful than a conventional interview or parliamentary debate occurred after the controversial sinking of the Argentine warship, the *General Belgrano* by the British navy in May 1982 during the Falklands War. While there was widespread public concern about the possibly illegal nature of this action, journalists had been uniformly reluctant to challenge the then British Prime Minister, Margaret Thatcher. In May 1982 Thatcher appeared on the *Nationwide* television program and agreed to take calls from the public. One call came from a housewife called Diane Gould:

> GOULD: Mrs Thatcher, why, when the *Belgrano*, the Argentinian battleship, was outside the exclusion zone and actually sailing away from the Falklands, why did you give the orders to sink it?
>
> THATCHER: But it was not sailing away from the Falklands – It was in an area which was a danger to our ships, and to our people on them.
>
> SUE LAWLEY: Outside the exclusion zone, though.
>
> THATCHER: It was in an area which we had warned, at the end of April, we had given warnings that all ships in those areas, if they represented a danger to our ships, were vulnerable. When it was sunk, that ship which we had found, was a danger to our ships.

My duty was to look after our troops, our ships, our Navy, and my goodness me, I live with many, many anxious days and nights.

GOULD: But Mrs Thatcher, you started your answer by saying it was not sailing away from the Falklands. It was on a bearing of 280 and it was already west of the Falklands, so I'm sorry, but I cannot see how you can say it was not sailing away from the Falklands.

THATCHER: When it was sunk . . .

GOULD: When it was sunk.

THATCHER: . . . it was a danger to our ships.

GOULD: No, but you have just said at the beginning of your answer that it was not sailing away from the Falklands, and I am asking you to correct that statement.

THATCHER: But it's within an area outside the exclusion zone, which I think is what you are saying is sailing away . . .

GOULD: No, I am not, Mrs Thatcher.

LAWLEY: I think we are not arguing about which way it was facing at the time.

GOULD: Mrs Thatcher, I am saying that it was on a bearing 280, which is a bearing just North of West. It was already west of the Falklands, and therefore nobody with any imagination can put it sailing other than away from the Falklands.

THATCHER: Mrs – I'm sorry, I forgot your name.

LAWLEY: Mrs Gould.

THATCHER: Mrs Gould, when the orders were given to sink it, when it was sunk, it was in an area which was a danger to our ships. Now, you accept that, do you?

GOULD: No, I don't.

THATCHER: I am sorry, it was. You must accept . . .

GOULD: No, Mrs Thatcher.

THATCHER: . . . that when we gave the order, when we changed the rules which enabled them to sink the *Belgrano*, the change of rules had been notified at the end of April. It was all published, that any ships that were, are, a danger to ours within a certain zone wider than the Falklands were likely to be sunk, and again, I do say to you, my duty, and I am very proud that we put it this way and adhered to it, was to protect the lives of the people in our ships, and the enormous numbers of troops that we had down there waiting for landings. I put that duty first. When the *Belgrano* was sunk, when the *Belgrano* was sunk, and I ask you to accept this, she was in a position which was a danger to our Navy.

LAWLEY: Let me ask you this, Mrs Gould. What motive are you seeking to attach to Mrs Thatcher and her government in this? Is it inefficiency, lack of communication, or is it a desire for action, a desire for war?

GOULD: It is a desire for action, and a lack of communications because, on giving those orders to sink the *Belgrano* when it was actually sailing away from our fleet and away from the Falklands, was in effect sabotaging any possibility of any peace plan succeeding, and Mrs Thatcher had 14 hours in which to consider the Peruvian peace plan that was being put forward to her. In which those 14 hours those orders could have been rescinded.

THATCHER: One day, all of the facts, in about 30 years time, will be published.

GOULD: That is not good enough, Mrs Thatcher. We need . . .

THATCHER: Would you please let me answer? I lived with the responsibility for a very long time. I answered the question giving the facts, not anyone's opinions, but the facts. Those Peruvian peace proposals, which were only in outline, did not reach London until after the attack on the *Belgrano*. That is fact. I am sorry, that is fact, and I am going to finish. Did not reach London until after the attack on the *Belgrano*. Moreover, we went on negotiating for another fortnight after that attack. I think it could only be in Britain that a Prime Minister was accused of sinking an enemy ship that was a danger to our Navy, when my main motive was to protect the boys in our Navy. That was my main motive, and I am very proud of it. One day all the facts will be revealed, and they will indicate as I have said.

LAWLEY: Mrs Gould, have you got a new point to make, otherwise I must move on?

GOULD: Just one point. I understood that the Peruvian peace plans, on a *Nationwide* program, were discussed on midnight, May 1st. If that outline did not reach London for another fourteen hours . . .

LAWLEY: Mrs Thatcher has said that it didn't.

GOULD: . . . I think there must be something very seriously wrong with our communications, and we are living in a nuclear age when we are going to have minutes to make decisions, not hours.

THATCHER: I have indicated what the facts are, and would you accept that I am in a position to know exactly when they reached London? Exactly when the attack was made. I repeat, the job of the Prime Minister is to protect the lives of our boys, on our ships, and that's what I did.

Worlds apart?

Thinking of the mass media as sacred space, we have attempted to show in this chapter how encounters between voices of the public and the media always possess a certain awkwardness caused by the fundamental asymmetry of power between producers and receivers. On odd occasions, a Diane Gould breaks into the well-managed sanctity of media space and disrupts the stability of authoritative voices. Recent election campaigns have been dramatized by moments of unplanned public intervention in stage-managed situations: for example, when politicians have lost their tempers with potential voters during campaign walkabouts, or are confronted by angry citizens whose lives have been affected by political decision-making such as health cuts, or when studio audiences refuse to clap political leaders. Sometimes these moments of media spontaneity are fatal for political authority, as when TV cameras focused upon the trembling hands of the Polish generals as they negotiated with the Solidarnosc trade unionists in 1989, or the crowd started to jeer at Ceausescu in Romania in 1991. But the drama of such occasions is precisely because they run counter to the norms and routines of media depictions of reality.

Some critics argue that these cracks in the edifice are too infrequent and hard to produce; that the media's relationship with the public is inevitably one of management and manipulation; that for the *demos* to be anything more than stage extras in the performance of democracy they must abandon hope of being acknowledged as serious contributors to an officially mediated conversation. Such critics turn instead to the prospect of alternative media as a space for public and counterpublic expression.

4

Counterpublics and Alternative Media

In the previous three chapters we have cast doubt upon the notion of a singular public, residing "out there in the world," waiting to be addressed as a homogeneous, potentially univocal collectivity. This notion is too simplistic and unhistorical, for it assumes that manifold modes of human association can be compressed into an indivisible citizenry or civic sphere. In rejecting the idea that an overarching conception of the public can fully capture the sociocultural complexity of collective action in any one society, one is acknowledging that all inclusive groups entail exclusions: that one can never designate a "people" without tacitly or otherwise designating non-members of that group as "others." As in "democratic" Athens, where the empowered *demos* excluded women, slaves, children, and immigrants, the "general public" can turn out to be far less all-embracing in reality than it is in rhetorical self-justification. It is in response to these preclusions, exclusions, and affronts that people who have been marginalized or discounted within "general" publics have formed counterpublics.

Used originally by Negt and Kluge[1] to challenge the bourgeois-dominated public sphere of Habermasian historiography, the term counterpublic was intended as a means of re-admitting the working class to its rightful place within the public. The term was later articulated by Felski[2] to further expand Habermas's conception of the public, this time to embrace not only women as a demographic group, but femininities as a sociocultural mode of civic behavior. Asen has provided one of the most concise and comprehensive definitions of counterpublics:

Counterpublics emerge as a kind of public within a public sphere conceived as a multiplicity. They illuminate the differential power relations among diverse publics of a multiple public sphere. Counterpublics signal that some publics develop not simply as one among a constellation of discursive entities, but as explicitly articulated alternatives to wider publics that exclude the interests of potential participants. Counterpublics in turn reconnect with the communicative flows of a multiple public sphere. Counterpublic theory discloses relations of power that obliquely inform public discourse and, at the same time, reveals that participants in the public sphere still engage in potentially emancipatory affirmative practice with the hope that power may be reconfigured. Such disclosure and revelation indicate the utility of "counterpublic" as a critical term. Serving in conceptual models and criticism of discourse in the public sphere, the term foregrounds contest among publics, exclusions in the discursive practices of publics, and attempts by some publics to overcome these exclusions.[3]

Counterpublics have a dialectical relationship to the "general" public, standing some distance away with a view to protecting, preserving, and nurturing their defining characteristics, while at the same time standing on the periphery with a view to infiltrating, influencing, and reconfiguring the wider entity upon which they are dependent as citizens. They are both outsiders and insiders; the other to a self-defined "us," forever seeking to encourage the "us" to become other than its hegemonically conceived self-characterization. This anti-hegemonic instinct of counterpublics has led to their being identified as emancipatory by nature. There is an expectation in liberal democracies that counterpublic voices will have opportunities to articulate alternatives to the norms and patterns of the dominant public. But, in reality, their capacity to do so via mainstream mass media is rather limited.

Campaigning groups and citizens have long endeavored to use mainstream media to make their positions and protests known, often resulting in what has been described as a dance in which the media rarely do other than take the lead, twirling campaigners around at will whilst retaining control over rhythm and pace. For example, in a study of the historic 1982 Franklin Dam blockade in Tasmania, which was one of Australia's most famous environmental protests, researchers found that in the early part of the protest, before each side began to battle for control over the media's representation of the event to the public, there was an interesting synchronicity between both sides. The friendliness of the initial relations between the two sides rapidly degenerated and although the "dance" resumed periodically over subsequent years, campaigners were rarely able to impact the media's stranglehold on the message or the image.[4]

Mainstream media are extremely reluctant to give much visibility to organizations which challenge or even threaten the political frames of the media agenda. Established advocacy organizations, such as Oxfam, fare a little better, but this is often at the cost of representing their causes in terms of moral sentiment rather than radical advocacy. Many campaign groups have become wary of courting mainstream media because of fears that their views will be distorted or ridiculed. Research studies have shown how mainstream media tend to characterize particular groups as blameworthy for particular social conditions or of holding extreme political views. In their influential series of studies of news media, the Glasgow University Media Group[5] documented the ways in which trade unions and strikers, for example, are represented almost exclusively from the point of view of elites such as politicians, industrial leaders, and company CEOs. The workers at the center of such stories are invariably portrayed as intransigent whingers intent on bringing their company to its knees through irresponsible actions such as strikes. Their voices are rarely heard at any length, but rather their actions are framed by narratives which reduce them to caricatures of noisy dissent.

Where campaign groups have tried more systematically to engage mainstream media, it has often been through stunts, marches, or events. It is perhaps ironic that by understanding and thus playing up to precisely the kind of story which will get mainstream journalists interested, activist groups can at least get their existence, if not their *raison d'être*, acknowledged by the mass media. Even if the story orientation might be less than favorable, in such circumstances the dictum that all publicity is good publicity is used to justify any bid for public recognition. The environmental campaigner and journalist, George Monbiot, argues that radical activists should not give up trying to spread their ideas through the mass media. He has written *An Activist Guide to Exploiting the Media* (available from the "The Land is Ours" website[6]) in which he provides advice to campaigners on skills such as how to write a press release. The site includes a virtual press room in which campaigners can then post their notices and journalists are encouraged to use the site to identify stories and sources.[7]

Playing the Media Game #1

Sarah Berger, a long-time peace campaigner cites a good example of a sit-up-and-notice "stunt" when, immediately prior to the G8 Summit in Genoa in 2001, the Italian government attempted to stop protesters entering the country and as a result, her own travel plans were summarily canceled by her booking agent. Her campaign group, the Brighton and Hove branch of the WDM (World Development Movement), issued a press release saying that the group intended traveling to Genoa in an inflatable dinghy and invited a photocall on Brighton beach. Coverage of the event, and of the campaign's viewpoint on the summit, was included in the BBC's prestigious flagship news and current affairs show, *Newsnight*, in what Berger describes as a "balanced" in-depth feature.[8] Berger also adds that she often uses her familial position as "grandmother" to attract media attention both as a strategy for visibility and as a way to show that "ordinary" women and men care about peace and the planet, not simply anarchists, and "grungies."

Playing the Media Game #2

The year after the G8 Summit in 2001, one of the UK's largest development charities, ActionAid, launched its "Dying for Diamonds" campaign, which included a Marilyn Monroe look-alike singing "Diamonds are a Girl's Best Friend" whilst holding a placard stating that 10,000 children in Sierra Leone have been abducted in order to be put to work in diamond mines.[9] Launching the campaign on the eve of the World Diamond Congress with the Marilyn stunt meant that the media covered the event, but also interviewed campaigners about the diamond trade and the "code of conduct" which they wanted the industry to adopt. Such coverage also conveyed the charity's main message to the public, that they should ask where diamonds come from.

The case studies show that the media will cover certain kinds of protest events made by "ordinary" people, but that such events need to conform to established notions of newsworthiness.

Alternatives to Mainstream Media

Rejecting these limited opportunities for exposure, many groups have chosen to develop their own alternative media forms. Alternative media have long provided a channel for diverse counterpublics to express themselves both to one another and to the "general" public. As the 1977 Royal Commission on the Press noted in response to the mushrooming of radical, underground publications in the 1960s and 1970s,

> The existence of an alternative press is important for two reasons. First, the right of minorities to publish their views without undue difficulty is at the heart of the freedom of the press. Second, one of the functions of the press in a democratic society is to reflect and impact the opinions of the widest range of articulate interests. A multiplicity of alternative publications suggests dissatisfaction with an insufficiently diverse established press, and an unwillingness or inability on the part of major publications to provide space for the opinions of small minorities.[10]

Of course, alternative media did not originate in the counter-cultural atmosphere of the 1960s. Alternative media forms are situational and historically grounded and respond to the issues of the day. For example, in the early nineteenth century the accessibility of the printing press as a relatively cheap way to produce written texts coincided with a newly radicalized political sensibility which was beginning to question established ideas about labor relations and conditions and the structure of political power. The coincidence of technology and politics produced an explosion of campaigning pamphlets, flyers, and newspapers which both called for social reform and ran satirical pieces which used humour to get across serious socio-political points.[11] The establishment response was, unsurprisingly, to harass publishers, make paper taxable, and imprison editors for writing or publishing "unacceptable" material. As the radical press found it increasingly difficult to survive, mainstream news publishers plundered their more popular characteristics, such as crime reports and social commentary, and incorporated them into their own formats. As advertisers were more keen to retain their respectability than be associated with radical alternatives to the mainstream, their support for the restyled populist press sounded the death knell for many radical publications.

Alternative media provide the means by which counterpublics can come to voice and engage in a public sphere in which the traditional media's gatekeeping proclivities are curtailed or ignored. Defining the characteristics of alternative media is far from simple. Various criteria have been formulated, such as media which promote views that run counter to or are openly hostile to the status quo; which are concerned with ideas rather than profits; in which content is determined by notions of social responsibility, including stories and issues which would not routinely appear in the mainstream media. Some definitions of alternative media point to the importance of their counter-cultural content; others place emphasis upon their democratic production process in which members of grass-roots communities or interest groups are empowered to become directly involved in media creation. Although the distinction is rarely as stark as we are presenting it, we might say that proponents of alternative media processes are more concerned to encourage communities to make their own news, tell their own stories, learn new skills, and foster community cohesion than in promoting a particular set of radical perspectives; while proponents of alternative media content endeavor to bring "ordinary" people into the media frame as subjects for stories through giving them voice.

A particularly useful way of thinking about the contours of alternative and radical media is offered by Atton who has developed a typology which incorporates both the process and content elements which combine to make alternative media genuinely different from the mainstream:

1 content – politically radical, socially/culturally radical; news values;
2 form – graphics, visual language; varieties of presentation and binding; aesthetics;
3 reprographic innovations/adaptations – use of mimeographs, IBM typesetting, offset litho, photocopiers;
4 distributive use – alternative sites for distribution; clandestine/invisible distribution networks; anti-copyright;

5　transformed social relations, roles, and responsibilities – reader-writers, collective organization, de-professionalization of, e.g., journalism, printing, publishing;
6　transformed communication processes – horizontal linkages; networks.[12]

In this model, alternative media is multi-faceted and each of the six dimensions can be more or less radical within the context of the whole; for example, a media channel could be radical in its organization, but conservative in terms of its intended audience; it might use only qualified journalists but within a structure that is non-hierarchical and inclusive; it could produce consistently counter-cultural content but have little direct accountability to its audience. In other words, alternative media should be seen as a set of practices which are fluid, overlapping, and complex, a hybrid and vibrant alternative to mainstream cultural production.

One of the key differences between alternative and mainstream media lies in the determination of what constitutes news and which voices should be represented in describing, explaining, and commenting upon the social events of the day. Alternative media politicize the otherwise hidden stories which lie beneath the surface of news items covered by the mainstream. The following sections of this chapter consider five forms of alternative media as channels of counterpublic representation.

The street and community press: a voice for the forgotten?

The Big Issue is probably one of the best known of all street newspapers and, following its early beginnings in the UK, versions of the newspaper are now to be found across Europe and beyond. Its rise can be seen as an explicit attempt to develop strategies of pointed advocacy for, by, and on behalf of street people. By functioning as both mouthpiece and conscience, street papers keep disparities of power between producers and readers, as well as between different types of reader, at the forefront of their journalism. In marked contrast to the mainstream media's construction of homelessness and poverty, usually by way of sensational stories about hypothermia and alcoholism, street newspapers tend to provide trenchant and informed critiques of social and economic inequities and how they impact on society's most vulnerable people. Importantly, these first-hand advocacy narratives are written in the authentic register of lived experience. Most of the street press adopt a philosophy which sits firmly within the "alternative" paradigm, publishing first-hand testimonies and everyday narratives experienced and produced by street people themselves. In their capacity as a lived voice for the unrooted poor, street papers provide a unique example of communicative democracy as they aim to reach out to a wider reading public and provide informed critique of prevailing social and economic injustice.[13] A distinguishing characteristic of street newspapers is that they encourage homeless and poor people to write content, but they actively recruit editorial board members from these same constituencies, thereby vesting editorial as well as journalistic power in a public that is rarely written about, occasionally written for, and hardly ever self-represented.

The Big Issue

The Big Issue was founded in the UK in 1991 to enable homeless people to help themselves by selling copies of the paper for their own profit. It was modelled on the example of *Street News* which was launched in November 1989 in New York. *Street News* was an experiment in cultural politics, intending to be partly community service, partly underground newspaper, and partly consciousness-raising. Uniquely, its founders appealed to the city's homeless community to contribute towards and distribute the newspaper, allowing vendors to keep a considerable proportion of the cover price and thus providing them with an income stream. Street newspapers as a genre are thriving, even if many are relatively short-lived: in 2000, the North American Street Newspaper Association could point to 50 publications across the United States.

By 1996 the *Big Issue* had a circulation of 500,000, which is considerably higher than many mainstream weekly papers.[14] By 1999, it had four regional issues in London, Wales, Scotland, and Northern England. It is now a highly professional enterprise, with copy written almost exclusively by journalists rather than homeless people and a strong editorial hand. Despite this nod towards commercial practice, *The Big Issue* is a success story if it continues to be considered as "alternative" and to offer a model to other countries facing similar problems of poverty and social exclusion. Whilst it now has a firm financial basis and could thus be seen as operating within a model of mainstream media, its forms of distribution are distinctly alternative and the kinds of interpersonal engagement which vendors (i.e. homeless people) have with those who stop and buy, could be seen as constituting precisely the kind of public dialogue which not only Habermas, but also Negt and Kluge, had in mind for their respective public and counterpublic spheres.

Like street newspapers, community newspaper have tended to be established by "ordinary" people with a keen sense or experience of community action and activism.

Honolulu Weekly

The *Honolulu Weekly* began publication in 1991 and was established by "Jane" in response to what she considered to be a need to provide an interesting alternative to the mainstream press and in particular, the two local dailies. Like most alternative newspapers, the *Honolulu Weekly* is without a stable financial basis, but Jane has been determined to make a viable business out of the newspaper. By 2003, it had a circulation of 45,000 at 24 different distribution outlets. It is a free sheet and covers its costs through a small group of local investors and advertising. Its owner-editor has a clear vision of what the newspaper offers:

a well-written product. Issues are covered differently at the *Weekly*. We pay attention to gay and lesbian issues and are concerned about being inclusive of a greater range of people in the community. We have an increased sensitivity to politics than other publications.[15]

The newspaper functions with a clear grass-roots orientation and its relative success and longevity suggests that it is possible to produce an alternative media product with an explicit ethical and counter-cultural agenda and remain solvent. Jane certainly believes that by exposing readers to a variety of views, especially on controversial topics, the newspaper can act as a genuine agent of change capable of shifting public opinion. Other staff at the newspaper also identify the newspaper's philosophy as being a particular attraction to working there, especially the fact that it is not afraid to speak out on important issues of local concern because there is no corporate proprietor to keep mollified. Whilst there is a permanent editorial team, the majority of articles are written by the 80+ freelancers who regularly contribute to the newspaper, few of whom are trained journalists. The roll-call of freelancers includes academics, environmentalists, human rights specialists, and other topic-specific experts. The newspaper also builds capacity amongst trainee journalists by taking on interns who are studying for journalism degrees. Less positively, though, the hard financial struggle for survival means that payments to staff are low and working conditions less advantageous than in mainstream news outfits, exacerbated by the fact that there is no union operating at the newspaper.

A brief overview of the *Honolulu Weekly* illuminates a tension between philosophy and practice, rhetoric and reality. Whilst owner-editor Jane promotes a counter-hegemonic critical discourse in the pages of her newspaper, the means by which she achieves this end could be seen as disadvantageous to the workers involved in its production. As with many enterprises which are rooted in the community and which rely on volunteer and untrained, albeit willing and enthusiastic, staff, alternative publications struggles to survive, largely due to precarious funding and a generally non-commercial approach to managing a "business." But of course such refusal to operate along commercial lines is a conscious decision for many organizations, precisely to reject the hierarchical contours of the mainstream and instead forge a new kind of media which is consciously egalitarian and avowedly committed to equality and change. They purposely operate within what is often called the "black and green" economy (after the colours of anarchy and environmentalism), so as to practice for themselves what they preach between their covers.

Zines as Sites of Resistance

Like other genres which are produced under the rubric of alternative media, "zines" (fan magazines) are marked out from the mainstream by both their mode and means of production. As with alternative media more generally, zine producers are amateur; their product is cheaply produced and hard copies are often distributed as photocopies; and the distinction between reader and writer is almost non-existent.[16] Importantly, zines have a social function beyond the mere provision of information: to open up spaces to different voices, to emphasize that the processes of production can be horizontal and sociable, and that the creation of media content can be a porous and open thing, not confined to so-called media professionals, but to all those who have a story to tell.

The content of zines is not always radical or alternative, but the fact that their producers are also their consumers, seeking to make something different for themselves as well as for others, marks them out as inherently democratizing. In particular, zines provide a channel through which children and young adults can find expression and speak to their peers as well as other audiences whose attention they would not usually reach. Zines produced by young women and girls have become sites of resistance through which they can challenge gender-based orthodoxies about what it means to be female in society, thus wresting some control away from the mass media and into their own hands. Importantly, the often anonymous voices of zine-writers enable difficult topics such as abuse and self-harm to be discussed in relative safety and also allow for a rehearsal of different identities in a non-judgmental context.[17] As zines often circulate within friendship circles and same-audience networks, they have the additional outcome of encouraging bonding within peer groups, building support around shared experience associated with being an almost-adult or otherwise on the "outside."

Community Broadcast Media: Bringing Communication Home

Early radio was produced by communities before it ever became controlled by states or corporations. Since the mid-1920s, grass-roots broadcasting has been squeezed from the spectrum, but a significant alternative broadcasting tradition does survive. Jankowski has identified the following features of community broadcast media:

- objectives: to provide news and information relevant to the needs of community members, to engage those members in public communication via the community medium; to empower the politically disenfranchized";
- ownership and control: often shared by community residents, local government, and community-based organizations;
- content: locally oriented and produced;
- media production: involving non-professionals and volunteers;
- distribution: via the ether, cable television infrastructure, or other electronic network;
- audience: predominantly located within a relatively small, clearly defined geographic region . . . ;
- financing; essentially non-commercial.[18]

Whilst most community or alternative media do not display all of these features, they are likely to all share some of them.

The development of community radio, described by Girard as "radio that encourages expression and participation, and that values local culture,"[19] has been particularly successful in parts of the developing world in which poor and marginalized groups would otherwise have no access to broadcast production because the costs of setting up commercial stations are too great for too little return. The development of community radio in the United States was rather slow but began a faster burn in the 1960s when fledgling community radio movement served as an incubator for citizens' voices to be broadcast to a wider listening public.[20] Campaigns by communities over the allocation of radio licenses to their local stations led to concerted campaigns against the proclivities of radio stations to ignore the interests of large parts of their local audience. This occasionally resulted in radio stations being denied a license to broadcast if they failed to change. Mostly, stations did enough to placate the complainants even if they did not embrace the diversity agenda with any real enthusiasm.

But the consequence was that local radio stations did become more sensitive to the importance of delivering content of interest to a wider listening audience. In the 1960s, government funding for start-ups and training as well as reductions in the cost of equipment meant that more people could get involved in setting up community radio stations themselves. The US Federal Communications Commission (FCC) took a very large step when it initiated its "preference policies" in the 1970s, resulting in many minority ethnic radio stations receiving licenses to broadcast. (Some of these are still broadcasting now, some three decades later.) This positive legal state of affairs was in stark contrast to the situation in which many small stations in the UK found themselves: because they were consistently denied the official licenses enjoyed by their US counterparts, they were forced to take to the seas as pirate radio stations, Radio Caroline being perhaps the most famous. Elsewhere in Europe, different national licensing authorities took a variety of approaches, but by the 1970s, community radio had a permanent place in the media landscape, either officially or as pirate entities, competing with the mainstream media.

KPFA Radio

One of the first community-access stations established in the United States was KPFA Radio based in Berkeley, California. It began broadcasting in 1994 and is funded through a combination of grants given by private organizations, such as the Ford Foundation, and via local fundraising activities. Although it now has paid staff, most people who work at KPFA (as in most other community-based media) are volunteers. It also houses the Pacifica Network which provides alternative and activist radio programming to other community-access radio stations in the USA.[21] As with other community-oriented stations, KPFA offers a diet of social commentary, politically oriented interviews, (non-mainstream) music, and news. Importantly, it offers internships to individuals from "under-represented" groups.[22]

Interviewed for a study of radio entrepreneurs,[23] the radio pioneer, Steve Dunifer, who has been a radio enthusiast since his teenage years, and now works to enable local communities to make radio programs for and about their local neighborhoods, explained his support for using whatever materials are to hand to create local media:

> One of the best and easiest applications is what we call drive-by radio. Almost every community has some sort of flea market in a public area or another type of event such as a festival. It is very easy to set up a small radio station (15 watt) on a table. Use a deep-cycle marine battery, which will power the transmitter all day. Put the antenna about 15 feet in the air with a tripod stand . . . hang banners and hand out flyers . . . telling people to tune to the frequency you are broadcasting on. Use a portable mixer with several microphones, a CD player and tape player. Encourage folks to go hold and bring their mix CDs or tapes to the table for airplay. Open up the microphone for impromptu shout-outs, raps, rants, etc. It is a great way to introduce the community to radio and get their involvement – real grassroots radio. This method works great for political actions as well, especially ongoing strike actions with picket lines and such.[24]

Whilst it is clear that some technical knowledge is required to set up even something as basic as a table-top radio station, it is nonetheless a good example of how communities can obtain a media voice in a corporate-dominated mass-communications environment. However, as Dunifer goes on to say, the pursuit of such activist media is vulnerable to political intervention by governments anxious about the proliferation of too many radical public voices. Not quite joking, he says he almost expects the FCC to "pass jurisdiction of unlicensed radio over to Home-land Security as a terrorist activity."

In a study of community radio stations in Australia, researchers found that three-quarters of broadcast news was local in focus.[25] Such localism means that community radio's fundamental aim to make programs of relevance to a local listening audience is met, as are several other ambitions besides: for example, to keep "connected" with local people and harness the talent of local "amateurs" to produce something genuinely different than the content available through mainstream media. From discussions with newsworkers in community radio, key sources for story ideas and copy are social conversations and their own network of contacts, as well as press releases and stories which have featured in the mainstream media. In other words, whilst some content is derived from national stories which are then given a local twist, most material is about local issues, so that community radio functions as a complementary rather than a replacement service to mainstream news. What counts as news for community radio is also often different to the principles which govern newsworthiness in mainstream media, so that the staples of the latter – conflict and celebrity – are much less important than proximity and local relevance. Once again, we see that differences in core values are important distinctions between community (and alternative) media and the mainstream, as are the relationships between producers and consumers, the ways editorial decisions are made, and the organizational structures within which media workers operate.

Women's Media

As with other alternative media, women's media activism began to become more consistent and visible in the 1960s and 1970s, not just in the United States, but around the world, often through the establishment of pirate radio stations. Women's desire to have their own interests reflected in radio content and to begin to construct their own images of themselves as part of a political counter-cultural campaign resulted in radically different shows emerging from stations such as Radio Donna in Rome, Les Nanas Radioteuses in Paris and Vrouwernradio in the Netherlands. A lesbian collective in Barcelona – Onda Verde – began producing programs in 1981. What differentiated women-run stations and women-produced content from programs made *for* women but *within* a mainstream broadcasting environment, was the extent of editorial control women had over content, thereby allowing them to tackle radical and controversial subjects without fear of being taken off the air. Women media activists were aware of the ease with which mainstream broadcasters could summarily axe programs aimed at women, on grounds not of low ratings but of editorial distaste. Mainstream media marginalization and even censorship of radical opinions provoked self-policing by program-makers under threat of contract withdrawal. Strong listener campaigns to save particular shows or programming segments and/or high ratings have often been the only way in which women have survived in otherwise hostile environments. This is what happened with *Frauenfunk* (Women's Radio) which aired for ten hours a week on Sender Freies Berlin during the 1990s and which had the highest audience ratings of any of the station's output, but where staff resisted persistent efforts by station management to "modify or eliminate the programming."[26]

The impetus for many feminists who wanted to get involved in specifically women-focused radio programming was primarily political: to use radio as a tool both for consciousness-raising and for progressing a feminist or at least women-oriented politics. For example, in 1987, Women's Scéal Radio[27] was the first low-powered neighborhood women's non-licensed autonomous radio station, broadcasting from Galway, in the Republic of Ireland. In its initial publicity, the station stated that it aimed to celebrate women's orality because it is women who pass on oral culture, and to enable free speech. Its publicity slogan pronounced "Free Women! Free the Air-Waves!" and invited all women to get involved. Finding ways in which women as a traditionally excluded category of "public" can come to voice through alternative media outlets was an important imperative underpinning the development of women's media, including community media.

Although short-lived, many women working in British community radio used the opportunity afforded by the restricted service licence (RSL), to showcase women's radio output during the 1990s. The RSL was a license to broadcast for up to 28 days each year as a way of developing production skills, learning how to set up and run a community radio station, and enabling challenging content to be aired.[28] These stations included: Fem FM (1992), Elle FM (1995, 1999), Radio Venus (1995, 1999), Celebration Radio (1994) and Brazen Radio (1994). Stations were often year-long experiments, run with a patchwork of funding and collaborators (e.g. local councils, universities, voluntary organizations) and culminating in a specific period of broadcasting. For example, Bridge FM was set up as a partnership between the University of Sunderland and a women's education project, the Bridge, and broadcast for one week during March 2000, to coincide with International Women's Day. Caroline Mitchell, who is actively involved in women's radio (a member of Fem FM) has suggested that these stations sought to provide a holistic approach to, "integrating training and programme-making, employing community development methods to reach women who might not have been aware of community radio."[29]

Finally, there remains a specific difference between alternative (women's) stations and "women's" programs within mainstream organizations. The fact of women's involvement in cultural production is no automatic determinant of a feminist orientation and in fact, some women, especially those working within the mainstream, deliberately eschew a feminist consciousness in the programs they produce. Addressing a female audience in ways which made radio feel more like a friend and which discussed topics of interest to women has been seen as more important than beating a feminist drum, even as the lack of a political engagement has been lamented. For example, Sally Feldman edited BBC Radio 4's flagship program for women, *Woman's Hour*, during the 1990s and voices her incredulity that before her stewardship, the program, "had managed to navigate the late 1960s and 1970s without paying undue attention to the advent of women's liberation or even the introduction of equal pay and equal opportunities legislation in the mid-1970s."[30] She argues that there was never any intention to inscribe the program with a "feminist ideology," but rather to place women and their interests first and to cultivate a female, if not feminist, perspective on everything, a strategy which she dubbed "twin peaks." Given that the show is now in its sixth decade of continuous broadcast (it first aired in 1946), it clearly serves a purpose and caters to an appreciative audience, perhaps precisely because it remains rosy rather than radical. The *Woman's Hour* team does, undoubtedly, have to constantly negotiate a minefield of compromise, not only because it is enclosed within the BBC and constantly scrutinized as "the woman's show" *par excellence*, but also because it needs to balance an exploration of the hard world "outside" with a celebration of the comfortable world of the domestic "inside."

Minority Ethnic and Indigenous Media

Whilst media produced by minority ethnic communities are an important part of the push to combat the unrelenting onslaught of monocultural, Eurocentric media, most independent channels are commonly under-financed and under-resourced, which means they find it hard to reach their target audiences. Despite the best of intentions, minority broadcast media often struggle to be heard even by loyal audiences desperate for imaginative content, because of limited airtime. Even radio stations

which have the luxury of a dedicated frequency often lack technical expertise and sophistication and are given space on the unpopular AM band
and at low power. Thus the potential for re-presenting different rendi-
tions of minority community life back to the communities concerned
is continuously thwarted by a lack of access to distribution outlets,
unstable radio frequencies, and expensive studio rental. Problems of distribution are compounded, ironically, by the staggering amount of choice
open to the audience as a consequence of digital technologies. Thus,
niche services such as those catering for discrete minority communities
become a mere note in the cacophonous din of electronic opportunities.

In an extended survey of minority ethnic media activities on several
continents, Browne found that minority media services are alive and thriving and display a disparate range of characteristics, including content,
motivation, and aspirations.[31] Because most stations broadcast to a discrete geographical area and are thus delivered locally, the participation
of the public is generally easy to organize, and although most rely on
external news feeds for a greater or lesser proportion of their content,
many also have phone-in and debate programs and music slots. In this
way, they actively encourage community participation through organizing
community forums, engaging local people in political discussion shows
during election time, and supporting local musicians.

But if, as with other non-mainstream media, indigenous and minority ethnic media aim to provide a particularly inflected kind of content
which is produced from within a specific community, how does its
content differ from its mainstream counterparts? And how does it deal
with events which affect members of its own community? In other
words, what makes it different and how impartial can and should it
be? One study which asked precisely this question focused on Native
American and mainstream US media coverage of a particular event. It
found that Native American print media was much more likely to use
their own writers to produce original news stories than mainstream
media, although it also found that Native American websites often
relied on mainstream news feeds and wire services.[32] This reliance on
mainstream material obviously raises questions about the reality of
the "alternative" being offered by some indigenous media. However,
despite the use of mainstream sources, all the Native American media
examined included material produced from within the community, so
the voices of tribal leaders were all the louder for having outlets from
which to speak. Moreover, the global reach of websites, despite the

relatively parochial nature of their content, as with a website such as Red Lake Net News, means that counter-hegemonic messages are disseminated globally and not just locally.

Other studies which have explored the contours of minority ethnic media show evidence of a thriving alternative sector.[33] For example, one Canadian mapping exercise revealed high levels of media run by and for ethnic minority communities, including 250 newspapers and 14 full-service radio stations. The country also boasts the first national public TV station targeted specifically at aborigine communities, Aboriginal People's Television, established in 1999. Minority media in Canada appear to function as a provider of alternative viewpoints to those expressed in the mainstream, particularly on topics relating to minority communities within Canada. Whilst the ethnic press is committed to covering "good news" stories about success within indigenous communities, it nevertheless does not shy away from dealing with controversial issues such as criminality. However, most outlets try and put such incidents in their socio-political context, not as justification but as background, and will often seek views from within the community in relation to possible resolutions.

The *Montreal Community Contact*

This newspaper was established in 1992 by Egbert Gaye and currently has a circulation of around 7,500. It's a free sheet and covers its costs through advertising and some grant funding. An analysis of random copies of the newspaper shows that it is interested in promoting black heritage and celebrating the success of black business people in the city and Canada more widely. Importantly, as with the Native American press, news content avoids mainstream media's proclivities of stereotyping tradition as quaint and irrelevant folklore, and instead reinscribes minority ethnic culture as meaningful within a contemporary context. Often stories are constructed using several linguistic tropes include patois and pidgin English as a conscious strategy of cultural authenticity and assertion of heritage and experience.[34]

However, despite the more positive coverage given to ethnic minority communities within the Montreal Community Contact, its poor distribution processes means that its impact on Montreal life is rather limited. This problem is not restricted to this particular newspaper but is a general problem for community newspapers, exacerbated in cases like this, where copies are usually left in shops and other outlets frequented by the target community. Without additional financial resources, it's hard to see how this situation might change, although a more sophisticated distribution network which utilizes the goodwill of supporters might enable a wider diversity of outlets to be targeted.

Beyond Counterpublic Enclaves

Arguably, the alternative media sector is able to maintain and sustain itself because its supporters, creators, producers, and consumers share a common belief in the wider "political" project of challenging the cultural status quo and expanding democratic space. However, the precarious financial basis of most alternative media projects, in both the developing and the developed world, means that the sector's aspirations will always exceed its reality. For example, most community stations are staffed by volunteers, not able to broadcast for more than a few hours each day, and are relegated to using the less popular AM band. So, despite the local relevance of geographically situated community media, or the topic-specificity of stations targeted at specific niche audiences such as women, minority ethnic communities, or the LGBT community, alternative media will always battle against the odds.

In the highly volatile and precarious landscape within which alternative and community media must function, it is perhaps naïve to expect ideology and politics to take precedence over broader, pragmatic issues of audience reach and message credibility. A fundamental task for alternative media, if they are not to become culturally ghettoized, is to move beyond the simple creation and reflection of counterpublics as audiences, producers, and consumers (important though this work is in enriching the communicative process) and to seek to expand the norms and practices of the public sphere. This presents alternative media with a dialectical challenge to transcend simple postures of defensive activism, in which counterpublics tend to write for and talk to themselves rather than engaging a wider audience, or peripheral mainstreaming, in which counterpublics accept a sidelined status within the general public sphere. Counterpublics are most likely to be successful when they mobilize diverse networks of social action with a view to enriching the pluralism of the public sphere. As we shall see in the next chapter, some media theorists regard the Internet as the most promising space for this to happen.

5

Virtual Publicness

Digital information and communication technologies (ICT) have inspired a giddy rhetoric of public empowerment. Consider the decision by *Time* magazine to award its prestigious "Person of the Year" title in 2007 to "You, the Public":

> We're looking at an explosion of productivity and innovation, and it's just getting started, as millions of minds that would otherwise have drowned in obscurity get backhauled into the global intellectual economy . . . Who are these people? . . . [W]ho actually sits down after a long day at work and says . . . I'm going to turn on my computer and make a movie starring my pet iguana? . . . Who has that time and that energy and that passion? The answer is, you do.[1]

For other cyber-enthusiasts, *Time*'s second-person pronoun was too distancing. Dan Gillmor's (2004) book, *We The Media*, declared that "technology has given us a communications toolkit that allows anyone to become a journalist at little cost and, in theory, with global reach."[2] In the same year, Bowman and Willis' *We Media: How Audiences Are Shaping the Future of News and Information*, asserted that "the audience has taken on the roles of publisher, broadcaster, editor, content creator (writer, photographer, videographer, cartoonist), commentator, documentarian, knowledge manager (librarian), journaler and advertiser (buyer and seller.)"[3] This promiscuity of personal pronouns echoed the ode to digital empowerment composed almost a decade earlier by John Perry Barlow, best known hitherto as the lyrics writer for the Grateful

Dead. In the "Declaration of the Independence of Cyberspace," Barlow proclaimed that

> We are creating a world where anyone, anywhere may express his or her beliefs, no matter how singular, without fear of being coerced into silence or conformity . . . Our identities may be distributed across many of your jurisdictions. The only law that all our constituent cultures would generally recognize is the Golden Rule. We hope we will be able to build our particular solutions on that basis. But we cannot accept the solutions you are attempting to impose.[4]

In this chapter we scrutinize the rhetoric of e-empowerment and consider the extent to which "the public" can be said in any meaningful sense to have taken control of global media, framed a new "digital" democracy, and created a world where anyone, anywhere, may express his or her beliefs, no matter how individualized. Hyperbolic and technologically determinist though such claims surely are, they reflect a pervasive early twenty-first-century belief about the transformation of publicness.

Five main claims have been advanced by scholars as evidence that digital media in general – and the Internet particularly – constitute a new, more potentially democratic media space. These are:

- by creating a condition of information abundance, digital media have disrupted elite dominance of knowledge production and dissemination and increased public access to a broad range of public information and knowledge;
- by making access to media technologies inexpensive and technically accessible, digital media have widened the range of sources of media content. Anyone can become a media producer; making public surveillance and accountability ubiquitous;
- digital media make it easier than ever before for people to form and join dispersed communication network which, in turn, can link easily to other networks, enabling publics to be formed across distances;
- the monological features of broadcasting, based upon an industrial model of one-to-many transmission from a center, has given way to an interactive, many-to-many communication environment in which all message senders can expect to receive messages back;

- new media spaces open up a possibility for sharing, comparing, and reflecting upon public views, experiences, and feelings. There is scope, at least potentially, to create spaces of public deliberation in which positions are not merely articulated and advocated, but revised and even integrated in response to exposure to others.

Given the well-rehearsed shortcomings of the print and broadcast media in relation to many of these democratic aspirations, it is hardly surprising that new media researchers have chosen to pay attention to these possibilities of normative realization. If digital media could be shown to open up spaces for publics to form, interact, be witnessed, and exercise influence upon the world around them, this would constitute a major democratic advance beyond the restrictive media environment discussed in previous chapters. In the remainder of this chapter we set out some of the arguments and evidence in support of the five claims for the potential of digital democracy, followed by some qualifying observations which give substance to a more cautious interpretation of the new media ecology. In conclusion, we offer some observations about the significance of new media in reconfiguring relationships between political and professional elites and the public.

Information Abundance

Traditionally, opportunities to access official information have been mediated by well-resourced gatekeepers. Because information has tended to be a scarce resource, elites have been in a position to control its content, cost, and flow. In the pre-digital environment citizens had to rely upon knowledge-producing centers, such as broadcasters and newspapers, for their accounts of social reality. From its inception, the Internet was seen as having potential to expand the range and depth of available public information, allowing people to access hitherto protected and costly data and broadening the spectrum of political, economic, and cultural voices capable of contributing to public knowledge. In his study of Internet effects upon American politics, Bimber argues that

New means for elites to distribute and acquire information, new possibilities for citizens to identify and communicate with one another,
changes in the ways that citizens interact with the news system, and
the historical preservation of information, among other developments,
contribute toward a state of *information abundance* in the political
system.[5]

Information abundance has three principal consequences for democratic culture. Firstly, it makes common knowledge freely available. The
Internet allows people to become searchers for information, often without knowing in advance what they need to know. Official accounts are
forced to compete with rumors, conspiracy theories, and parodies. In an
information environment characterized by the production of more
online data every ten days than the entire volume of books collected in
the University of Oxford's Bodleian Library over six centuries,[6] trusted
interpreters become more important than ever.

Political institutions respond to information abundance by releas-
ing official data with a view to gaining public trust. For example, in
December 2006 the UK's Lord Chancellor's Department launched a
Statute Law Database, including all primary legislation. Lawyers had long
had access to similar information resources, but, by placing this online
at no cost to users, the British government effectively made its laws into
a public good (what economists call an externality), access to which could
not be denied to anyone on the basis of cost or copyright. The effect
of augmenting the store of publicly accessible common knowledge is
both material – it becomes a resource to be used – and cultural, in that
transparency comes to be regarded as the norm. In societies where
there is a high degree of governmental or commercial corruption, making information such as procurement and license applications transparent
has made life significantly easier for citizens and harder for dishonest
officials.

Secondly, in a world where information is both abundant and easy
to challenge, citizens are less likely to respond passively to what they
are told by authorities. They are increasingly inclined to comment
upon, personalize, or even remix information in ways that make most
sense to themselves. The remix – or mash-up – culture of music fans,
who digitally recombine and revise sounds to suit their own tastes, has
now spread into other spheres.

TheyWorkForYou

TheyWorkForYou is a site launched in 2004 by independent social hacktivists with the aim of aggregating content from the official reports of the proceedings of the British Parliament (*Hansard*) so that they could be more accessible to the lay public. The site (http://www.theyworkforyou.com) allows users to track a particular issue or Member of Parliament, comment on parliamentary proceedings, and register for regular updates on selected themes. The TheyWorkForYou model changes the terms of democratic visibility, using digital technologies to establish a citizen-centric, needs-based approach to parliamentary transparency. This marks a break with institutionally managed approaches to political communication that have hitherto dominated parliamentary information systems and could, if allowed to develop, lead to a greater degree of public understanding and ownership of the legislative process.

Thirdly, as it has become possible not only to receive information, but also to produce and disseminate one's own accounts, images, and explanations, innovative practices of collaborative online knowledge-making have mushroomed. The best example of this has been the rise of Wikipedia, an online encyclopedia that anyone can edit. Users employ a technology known as a "wiki" to allow visitors to the site to add, remove, edit, and change available entries, easily and quickly. Previously, online collaborative systems were the preserve of specialist or professional communities. By opening up Wikipedia to global collaboration, without epistemological gatekeepers determining who is qualified to contribute to public knowledge, the site has become immensely popular (it has nearly 700 million visitors annually, over 10 million articles comprising over 1.7 billion words and operates in 253 different languages) and serves as a model for what Bruns has called "produsage," a term which "highlights that within . . . communities which engage in the collaborative creation of information and knowledge . . . the role of 'consumer' and even that of 'end user' have long disappeared, and the distinctions between producers and users of content have faded into comparative insignificance."[7] Without needing to go all the way with Bruns in assuming that these trends in knowledge production herald a post-industrial order, it is clearly the case that decentralized, distributed ways of describing the world constitute a formidable challenge to informational gatekeeping.

A direct consequence of the expansion of available mediaspace, counterpublics find it easier than in the past to circulate accounts intended to gain a public hearing for their versions of social reality. For example, people accused of civil or criminal offenses, who are rarely invited to express their points of view in the mainstream media, often feel that their actions represent a higher justice than that accepted by the legal system. In previous centuries they would have had to resort to publishing leaflets and ballads (often illegally) in the hope of winning public attention, but now the adoption of online strategies can undermine the state's powerful hold on definitions of justice.

McSpotlight

Helen Steel and Dave Morris were the defendants in Britain's longest-ever libel trial against the McDonalds chain (1990–1997) and on February 16, 1996, outside one of the chain's outlets in Leicester Square in London, they launched the McSpotlight website,[8] using a borrowed laptop and a mobile phone. A press conference at a local Internet café generated significant media interest and the website registered 35,000 hits within its first 24 hours of operation. In a subsequent interview, Morris argued that "the imaginative and determined efforts of those involved with McSpotlight were an additional dimension, a real boost and an absolute winner."[9] Within three years of the McSpotlight site going live and a year before the final verdict came in, the site had claimed 65 million hits[10] and some of these visitors would have been journalists pleased to have found a one-stop-shop to source material for their stories.

The huge repository of materials contained on the website could be daunting for the novice visitor, but the creation of the site by "ordinary" people such as Steel and Morris means that it is user-friendly and easy to navigate.

While creating unprecedented opportunities for groups and individuals to produce and distribute their own counter-narratives and alternative forms of knowledge, the Internet has also given rise to new ways of describing, collating, and tagging the mass of online data from which "useful" information can be selected. Where there are only a few information sources to choose from, decisions about what to trust tend to rely upon institutional reputations. In a condition of global information abundance, where news, product descriptions, political leaks, opinions, and rumors are continuously being produced and circulated, often without their sources being clear, the capacity to filter relevant, meaningful, and accurate content becomes vital. Information about information (or metadata) is captured online through strategies of tacit and explicit collaboration. Processes in which users tacitly collaborate in determining the status of content through the use of search engines and other page-ranking tools are those in which countless acts of searching for web content, buying books, or browsing news stories are mined for the purpose of capturing metadata with a view to ranking sites. As Benkler has observed, "Google's strategy from the start has been to assume that what individuals are interested in is a reflection of what other individuals – who are interested in roughly the same area . . . think worthwhile."[11] By developing algorithms that detect common patterns of search destination and linkage, Google is able to model its metadata empirically, claiming that whichever site comes at the top of the list when one searches for "Zimbabwe" or "freedom" reflects the cumulative practices of all previous browsers who set out with the same inquiry. A second, more transparently intentional means of capturing metadata is for individuals to contribute explicitly to information-sharing networks such as del.icio.us or flickr or reddit. This form of social tagging employs techniques of networked annotation to give meaning to online ontologies. As Shirky argues, this presents a significant challenge to traditional knowledge hierarchies:

> Does the world make sense or do we make sense of the world? If you believe the world makes sense, then anyone who tries to make sense of the world differently than you is presenting you with a situation that needs to be reconciled . . . If, on the other hand, you believe that we make sense of the world . . . then you don't privilege one top level of sense-making over the other . . . Critically, the semantics here are in the users, not in the system.[12]

A particularly interesting development in the evolution of social tagging is IssueCrawler software, developed by the Amsterdam-based Govcom Foundation (www.issuecrawler.net). This searches for and maps themes, groups, and their interconnections, sometimes illuminating discrete communication links that would not be accessible through micro-analysis.

None of this is to suggest that the balance of informational power has swung away from elites. It is still the case that most people receive their information from the mass media and that the most popular online news sites receive their feeds from a small group of well-resourced corporate agencies. But the information ecology has changed; online formats from blogs and wikis to YouTube videos and email lists constitute pluralistic cracks in the edifice of centralized news production.

Surveillant Accountability

In 1948 the television series, *Candid Camera*, initiated a tradition of using concealed cameras to expose the reactions of "ordinary people" to unusual situations. The show remained popular for many years, framed by the simple broadcasting juxtaposition between the camera's centrally controlled gaze and the public's guileless vulnerability. As cameras, skills, and other technologies of surveillance and distribution have been simplified and made more widely available, with the emergence of digital cameras, portable email, blog software, and microrecorders, the locus of media production has begun to shift from professional centers to the dispersed public.

The video-sharing site, YouTube, is the *Candid Camera* of the digital era. Established in 2005, the site hosts approximately 90 million videos, the vast majority of which are made by non-professional producers seeking to give publicity to themselves, their friends, strangers, or recognized figures. Unlike *Candid Camera*, which assumed it was addressing a homogeneous public, amused by the obviously ridiculous, outraged by the manifestly offensive, and entranced by the mishaps which served to affirm the natural order, YouTube is a polysemic text. Fiske's notion of "semiotic democracy"[13] in which audiences are creatively involved in the construction of cultural symbols, rather than receiving them as passive consumers, is helpful in explaining how YouTube, as well as many other user-generated content sites, open up a space for anyone to submit content and anyone to ascribe meaning to it. In contrast to the division of creative labor inherent to broadcast media, in which, according to Arnison, there is a "natural hierarchy" which exists between storytellers and their audiences because the "storyteller has access to some piece of technology, such as a TV transmitter or a printing press,"[14] digital media militate against assumptions that most people aren't very creative and that it is only natural for just a few people to tell stories to the many.

As the public has come to be the collective subject of surveillance (there is one CCTV camera for every 14 people in Britain), counter-surveillance has come to be seen as an act of democratic resistance. While there is by no means a parity of resources between the major media institutions and individual citizens, this does mean that the public, as a collectivity, possesses a hitherto unavailable capacity to observe, scrutinize, expose, challenge, and ridicule those who were hitherto able to operate within secluded and privileged spaces of self-defined privacy. This has taken three main forms, each of which is illustrated by examples below.

Firstly, the candid gaze of the public disrupts the capacity of politicians, celebrities, and power-wielders to indulge in the luxury of invisibility. With increasing frequency, actions and aspects of elite personas are exposed to unintended public attention, thereby undermining the mystique of their well-rehearsed charisma and authority. Thompson refers to this changed balance of communicative power as "the new visibility":

> Whether they like it or not, political leaders today are more visible to more people and more closely scrutinized than they ever were in the past; and at the same time, they are more exposed to the risk that their actions and utterances, and the actions and utterances of others, may be disclosed in ways that conflict with the images they wish to project. Hence the visibility created by the media can become the source of a new and distinctive kind of *fragility*. However much political leaders may seek to manage their visibility, they cannot completely control it. Mediated visibility can slip out of their grasp and can, on occasion, work against them.[15]

Arrangements for event-staging, impression management and opinion measurement, which had assumed the role of quasi-scientific techniques of control in the broadcasting era, have been seriously disrupted by the slipperiness of the new mediated visibility has become more slippery for elites to manage. The fate of US Senator George Allen is but one episode in a growing catalogue of exposures of political leaders by media-equipped citizens.

The Case of Senator George Allen

While campaigning for re-election, Virginia Senator George Allen was regularly followed by a young man named S.R. Sidarth, who was working for the campaign of his challenger, Jim Webb. Sidarth's role was to record Allen's public appearances on video, in order to capture everything he said publicly, in case it could be used by the Webb campaign. On a campaign visit in August of that year, Allen publicly acknowledged Sidarth's presence to participants at the rally, referring to Sidarth on two occasions as "Macaca." Sidarth, who is of Indian descent, posted the video clip of Allen's comments on youTube and other Web sites, where it was soon viewed by hundreds of thousands of Internet users. Soon the video became a major campaign issue, as Allen had to fend off charges that the word "macaca," which is a genus of primate, was used in a racially derogatory way. Allen apologized and maintained that the word held no derogatory meaning to him. Later that November, Allen lost his reelection bid by a narrow vote, and many commentators speculated that the user-generated content shot by Sidarth played a role in Jim Webb's defeat of Allen.[16]

A second form of democratic surveillance has occurred at the level of the exercise of once secretly conducted state power. The publicity given to cellphone videos of prisoners being tortured, taken for their own pleasure by US servicemen at Abu Ghraib prison in Iraq, are perhaps the most infamous example of how the course of a war, supported by a sophisticated propaganda machine, could be destabilized by unwanted visibility. But this is not the only example of state abuses being captured and subjected to public attention as a result of digital media.

Thirdly, there are powerful examples of digital media being used by people to record and bear witness to their own lives and environments. The blogosphere is replete with accounts of what it feels like to be in a war zone, a hierarchical workplace, a political dictatorship, or at a pop festival, for example. Digital storytelling, as a genre which fuses the biographical intimacy of self-disclosure with the universal publicity of a call for attention, blurs boundaries between the personal and the political, the testimonial and the advocative, the linear and the fragmented. "It aims not only to remediate vernacular creativity but also to legitimate it as a relatively autonomous and worthwhile contribution to public culture."[17] Unlike *Candid Camera* or *vox pop* interviews, in which the words and actions of the public are always the object of professionally determined narratives and scenarios, digital media allow individuals and communities to focus upon themselves, intentionally and reflexively, with a view to making their own sense of who they are and what they do.

Urban Tapestries

Urban Tapestries investigated how, by combining mobile and Internet technologies with geographic information systems, people could "author" the environment around them; a kind of Mass Observation for the twenty-first century. Like the founders of Mass Observation in the 1930s, we were interested in creating opportunities for an "anthropology of ourselves" – adopting and adapting new and emerging technologies for creating and sharing everyday knowledge and experience; building up organic, collective memories that trace and embellish different kinds of relationships across places, time, and communities.[18]

The reference to Mass Observation is interesting. In Chapter 1, we quoted Pickering and Chaney's description of this movement as an attempt "to socialise the means of documentary production by providing ordinary people with a channel through which they could communicate what went on around them, within the ambit of their day-to-day lives."[19] In reality, the project was to observe the public, following in the footsteps of Victorian urban explorers such as James Greenwood, George R. Sims, and Jack London, who ventured into the slums to watch the insecurities and indignities of others. Being watched, whether under the authoritarian arrangements of the utilitarian panopticon or the benign condescension of quasi-sociology, is qualitatively different from seeing one's world through one's own eyes. Just as

YouTube undermines the privilege of media centers, Urban Tapestries subverts the notion of observation as examination from a distance.

Dispersed Networks

In early writing about the Internet, researchers speculated that it might open up new spaces of virtual sociability and association, lowering costs of entry to collective action and diminishing the cues that have traditionally inhibited the emergence of cross-cutting social networks. Such optimism was countered by other early studies which claimed that Internet use tended to distract people from social and civic participation. For example, Kraut et al. concluded that "Like watching television, using a home computer and the Internet generally implies physical inactivity and limited face-to-face social interaction."[20] Indeed, they found Internet users to be prone to loneliness and depression. Similarly, Nie and Erbring[21] claimed to find a relationship between frequent Internet use and social isolation.

In opposition to these negative accounts of the democratic potential of the Internet, other scholars have produced strong empirical evidence to suggest that citizens can derive increased social capital from the experience of interacting online. These researchers have found that the Internet does not simply support people in their existing social activities, but "contributes to the development of new communication formats which modify existing activities as well as help[ing[[to] shape new activities."[22] Quan-Haase and Wellman have examined extensively the relationship between online networks and social capital and conclude that "the Internet occupies an important place in everyday life, connect-ing friends and kin both near and far. In the short run, it is adding on to – rather than transforming or diminishing – social capital."[23] In a separate study, Wellman et al argue that online networks empower individuals rather than groups or communities (they refer to this phenomenon as "networked individualism") by enabling them to personalize their associations:

> Each person is a switchboard, between ties and networks. People remain connected, but as individuals, rather than being rooted in the home bases of work unit and household. Each person operates a separate

personal community network, and switches rapidly among multiple sub-networks.[24]

Kavanaugh and Patterson, on the basis of a three-year study of the Blacksburg Electronic Village, and Krieger and Muller, based on their study of chatroom and newsgroup participants, endorse the findings of Wellman et al. that being part of an online network enhances citizens' reciprocity, solidarity, and loyalty.[25] All of these studies stress the fact that online networks are not self-contained communities in which people retreat from face-to-face physicality, but an extension of and supplement to the world of offline interactions.

In contrast to these definitive claims for and against the Internet-sociability hypothesis, a more recent third wave of Internet researchers have arrived at a more nuanced position, dismissing the notion of the Internet as a single, amorphous medium that is used in undifferentiated ways, and rejecting the idea of a uniform experience for Internet use. Users of the Internet, like viewers of television, are driven by a range of motives and expected gratifications. It is only by exploring patterns and purposes of Internet use that meaningful civic effects can be established. On the basis of such a uses and gratifications study, Shah et al. found that

> individuals who use the Internet for information exchange probably encounter more mobilizing information and experience more opportunities for recruitment in civic life. Indeed, with the panoply of mobilizing content available on-line, citizens who are armed with such information may be able to exert greater control over their environments, encouraging participation and enhancing trust and contentment. Further, with e-mail comes the opportunity to connect with others, organize activities and recruit volunteers – all of which should increase the individual-level production of social capital.[26]

But this only applies to those Internet users who seek and exchange online information, since these researchers also found that "use of the Internet for social recreation appears to diminish the production of social capital, especially the psychological components of the construct."[27] This is supported by Johnson and Kaye's study which sought to establish "how well motivations for using the Internet predict online activities and, in turn, how well online activities predict Internet gratifications after controlling for demographics, time spent online, and level of perceived Internet expertise."[28] They found that "politically interested web users were motivated to go online for different reasons than the general public . . . and therefore they participated in different activities online." These are interesting conclusions, insofar as they help to explain relationships between expressly political motives and online behavior. But, as we shall argue in the next chapter, the line between recreation and information exchange is not necessarily as obvious as political scientists might suggest. Indeed, it may well be within online networks that eschew a political identity that publics are most likely to be formed and public affairs influenced.

While doubt remains as to how far online networks encourage inclusive or cross-cutting sociability, it is clearly the case that they can support modes of informal collaboration which transcend the logic of centrifugal organization. Bennett's claim that "the distributed (multi-hub or polycentric) structure of the Internet somehow causes contemporary activists to organize in remarkably non-hierarchical, broadly distributed and flexible networks"[29] is supported by the following examples of the Internet appearing to facilitate decentralized forms of collective action.

Kikass

Neil Almond, the chief executive of the youth charity, Kikass, says that the Internet and mobile phones have enabled his organization to organize:

> It's primarily a networking vehicle because it enables us . . . to have communication. We can have online "brainstormings." We can do things a lot quicker as well. So it means that whereas traditionally it might have taken two weeks to do something, we could have perhaps consulted with the forty young people we needed to in twenty-four hours or get two hundred responses within twenty minutes. One of the advantages of working online is that it gives the power to the individual rather than the organization, and . . . having that power creates a sense of responsibility and a better buy into the organization, it's more of a choice.

The Internet, and modern technology, has this amazing potential to tap into by get people involved in decision-making. Now, I think there's responsibility that needs to go with that. And also I think that that shouldn't be a scary thing for politicians, because I think it actually makes their job easier. You know, it's possible for us to get the views of one thousand young people in a matter of half an hour or an hour, which is really important for our decision-making process . . . I think that that's the opportunity of e-democracy: people who currently have to make decisions based in a vacuum can actually consult on those issues, but, more than that, can actually work-up, probably, better solutions that would work for people and perhaps also get beyond the political activists, for instance, a politician consulting with a group of young people.[30]

Leeds University Students Union Shows How A Facebook Network Mobilized Protesters

The protest was about a landlord who had been accused of holding tens of thousands of pounds in deposits from student households. A group was set up in order to help students take matters into their own hands. The group took direct action in an attempt to highlight that although the landlord's letting business had been closed down, he still had links with new and existing letting agents who may behave in a similar way.

Facebook was used to contact people on Facebook groups who openly exhibited a dissatisfaction with student landlords. Despite the fact that members of the 75 student households who had all had trouble with the specific landlord targeted by the campaign were emailed about the meeting directly, when a meeting was held to organize an action, 24 out of the 25 people in attendance were there having heard about it on Facebook. Facebook is now the primary method of communication between members of the group.[31]

EZLN

On New Year's Day 1994, around 3.000 Indian peasants from Chiapas declared themselves as the Ejército Zapatista de Liberación Nacionale (EZLN) and as their armed struggle began, a figurehead, in the shape of "Subcommander Marcos" emerged. Early on in the campaign, Marcos established an online presence and almost immediately a global network of websites, email listservs and Usenet discussion lists erupted which resulted in intense media interest and the arrival of hundreds of journalists into Chiapas to report on the uprising. Within two weeks, the Mexican President, Carlos Salina de Gortari declared a cease-fire and opened up negotiations with EZLN. Whilst the jury is out on exactly who was behind the development and funding of the various online activities which supported the EZLN, what is not in doubt is the role that online communication played in at least bringing the media spotlight to a part of the world which is routinely ignored. The spectacularly successful exploitation of the Internet by a group which would never be allowed mainstream media airtime demonstrates the changing nature of political participation and the way in which local concerns can receive global attention and support. In that moment, the Zapatistas crystallized the beginning of a seismic shift in the way in which social movements could practice their politics, could activate and animate their supporters.[32]

In all three of the above examples groups went online with a view to consolidating their identity and making their presence felt as a public. In short, these were not attempts by existing publics to affirm or advocate known positions, but exercises in making a claim to publicness through the visibility of association. It is this capacity not only to connect with others, but to be witnessed as a public that makes online networks particularly promising from a democratic perspective.

Many-to-Many Conversation

From its earliest days, the monological character of mass broadcasting was subjected to critical interrogation. Brecht famously argued that "The radio would be the finest possible communication apparatus in public life . . . if it knew how to receive as well as to transmit, how to let the listener speak as well as hear, how to bring him into a relationship instead of isolating him."[33] As we have shown in previous chapters, while many broadcasters have recognized the limitations of what Postman has called "the one-way conversation,"[34] attempts to produce "interactive content" have been constrained by asymmetries of power and a reluctance on the part of media insiders to surrender their hold upon the sacred space of message production. From its outset as a public network, the Internet's inherent feedback path has raised hopes amongst some commentators as to its capacity to become an unprecedentedly polylogical communication medium, more like a public telephone wire than centrally produced television. The promise of many-to-many conversation overriding the hegemonic output of the broadcasting industry has aroused hopes of a more inclusively democratic public culture in which the ability speak and be heard would not be dependent upon ownership or control of elaborate and costly resources.

Digital interactivity operates in two directions: vertically and horizontally. Vertical interactivity occurs when established message transmitters – broadcasters, newspapers, politicians, companies – invite the public to "talk back" to them. The communication path is linear and controlled: we speak; you respond. For example, politicians, used to making speeches directed at mass audiences whose main means of responding is to clap, boo, or cheer, have utilized digital feedback paths as a means of establishing the semblance of direct communication with voters. The aim has been to evade the intermediary role of journalists and create something resembling a "conversation" with the people they represent. (The resemblance often breaks down at the point when the call and response of conversational turn-taking is rejected and interaction is felt to be staged or managed rather than naturally occurring.) In their study of three senior politicians' blogs, Coleman and Moss quote their stated reasons for adopting this form of communication.[35] European Commissioner, Margot Wallström states that

> I started to write a blog because I thought it offered opportunities that other media do not. It allows me to speak directly to some citizens that I would probably never have the opportunity to meet and to get their views directly back. (2.28.07)

British government minister, David Milliband's blog is headed by the following statement of purpose:

> This blog is my attempt to help bridge the gap – the growing and potentially dangerous gap – between politicians and the public. It will show what I'm doing, what I'm thinking about, and what I've read, heard or seen for myself which has sparked interest or influenced my ideas. (3.23.07)

Conservative Party leader, David Cameron, states in one of the his first video entries that

> I want to tell you what the Conservative party is doing, what we're up to, give you behind-the-scenes access so you can actually see what policies we're developing, the things that we are doing, and have that direct link . . . (9.30.07)

Although not all cases of vertical interactivity fall short of authentic dialogue, they tend to have more the flavour of a question-and-answer session than a free-flowing public discussion. Citizens addressing politicians, government agencies, or corporations via their blogs are invited to respond to top-down messages rather than to proactively set their own agendas or initiate dialogue with other citizens. This inevitably weakens the potential for spontaneous and autonomous communication, leaving intact the power of traditional agenda-setters and policy-makers.

In contrast, horizontal interactivity allows peer-to-peer communication to take place, thereby reconfiguring the role previously accorded to mass audiences. However active media audiences were conceived as being in the pre-digital era; their capacity to act upon texts was always qualified by their constrained position as receivers. However energetically the role is performed, to be a member of an audience is to be excluded from the primary locus of creative production. Digital "audiences," as they were persistently labelled in the earliest days of the World Wide Web, are qualitatively more active than receivers of mass-media because they are able not only to act upon the messages that are sent to them, but to re-address them to others whose presence in the interaction may well change the nature of the communication event. It therefore makes no sense to speak of users of email, Facebook, or online communities as message audiences. They are something else – and that qualitative change is a consequence of horizontal interactivity.

At the micro-level, horizontal interactivity serves to widen the scope of interpersonal communication. In a longitudinal study, Shklovski et al. found that email users are likely to have increased offline contact with people they know because they use it to arrange face-to-face meetings in which weak relationships might be strengthened.[36] Boase and Wellman argue that email is a particularly good method of one-to-one communication in a network society which connects disparate publics who are otherwise unknown to each other.[37] In short, although there is little evidence to suggest that going online makes people more or less sociable, it does reconfigure sociability, even in the offline world.

Turning to the macro effects of horizontal interactivity, the Internet provides geographically dispersed groups of people, who only came together hitherto as targeted addressees of centralized messages, to address one another on their own terms. For example, Power et al. note that,

> Improvements and additions to existing technology have made it possible for Deaf people to interact with a wider group of people and have global contact. Breivik (2005), for example, found that Norwegian Deaf people were using e-mail and the Internet to both interact more with hearing people and to establish "transnational" connections with Deaf people around the world.[38]

Football fans, who began in the 1970s to publish unofficial fanzines in which views about their clubs, communities, and the wider ramifications of the sport were aired, have gathered in large numbers on online message boards to exchange views on a range of issues well beyond the confines of last week's match.[39] Mothers with small children have formed an online network comprising 300,000 subscribers, in which they share knowledge and experiences about parenting.[40] Some local communities have achieved closer social bonds through the use of online networks.

Large-scale online discussions attract vast numbers of active participants, producing patterns of interactivity ranging from message-seeding to intense participation to occasional posting. For example, the

BBC's online message boards receive tens of thousands of messages each month; in the first month of the war in Iraq 350,000 postings were emailed to the site. The risk, of course, is that participants in a "conversation" of such a magnitude could easily become lost in a data smog of competing appeals to their attention. How can sense be made of such large-scale communicative interactions? One promising answer is to visualize or map the data so that its patterns of meaning are graphically represented to those who lack the time, energy, or ability to consider every single interaction. Buckingham-Shum, a pioneer of such techniques, argues that,

> Discourse tools provide a way to move fluidly between the different minds: a way to provide representational scaffolding for disciplined modelling, but permitting the creative breaking of patterns when needed and the forging of new syntheses; a way to show respect for diverse stake-holders' concerns by explicitly integrating them into the conversation; a way to bring into an analysis "messy" requirements such as ethical principles, as well as hard data and constraints.[41]

The critical question here is whether traditional problems of scale and coordination can be overcome by techniques of searching, structuring, and summarizing mass conversations. Just as social tagging has served to render vast volumes of information more meaningful by sharing the task of ascribing meaning to them, large-scale peer-to-peer communication requires techniques enabling people to stretch the bounds of the interpersonal. Some of these techniques are being developed through research on visualization and argument-mapping:

> In principle the "Conversation Map" system can be used just like a usual electronic news or mail program . . . The main difference is that the Conversation Map system analyzes the content and the relationships between messages and then uses the results of the analysis to create a graphical interface.[42]

The key advances in twentieth-century communication technologies involved enabling large numbers of people to be reached by message producers. It may be that the most important development in communication technologies in this century will involve the capacity to hear, organize, summarize, and acknowledge the voices, arguments, and moods of large numbers of people.

Preference Shifting

Of all the claims made for digital media, the most ambitious relate to the potential for online deliberation. Several scholars have suggested that the Internet might open up a space for the public to engage in meaningful and consequential political talk about matters of common and contested concern. For political theorists in the tradition of Arendt and Habermas, the existence of a public sphere in which opinions can be articulated, disputed, and acted upon is an essential normative foundation for democracy. Even if digital media can make information more abundantly accessible, the activities of the powerful more visible, collective action less costly and more efficient, and communication more dialogical, these effects would not in themselves change the way that people think or speak about their interests, preferences, and values. Only when these positions can be brought out into the open and made the subject of unconstrained public debate do they become truly political. Political talk "transforms subconscious sentiments into conscious cognition and provides the basis for an active rather than a passive political involvement."[43] Unlike democratic aggregation, which counts and structures public interests and preferences on the assumption that these are fixed and immutable, deliberation starts from the assumption that all preferences are potentially changeable and that preference-shifting is most likely to be a consequence of an open exchange of ideas.

The advent of the Internet was regarded by many scholars as providing a potential space for the kind of many-to-many deliberative interaction that has been so conspicuously missing from most political democracies. Blumler and Coleman argued that a "conspicuous weakness in twentieth-century representative democracies has been the absence of robust public deliberation" and that the Internet possesses a "vulnerable potential" to "improve public communications and enrich democracy."[44] A number of ad hoc deliberative exercises have been initiated in the past decade, ranging from online parliamentary consultations[45] to trans-European policy debates.[46] Experiments have been conducted with a view to understanding how people deliberate online and whether political institutions are open to interactive input. There is some evidence to suggest that the Internet, as an environment characterized by low-cost entry, large volumes of accessible information and asynchronous interactivity, is well-suited to forms of inclusive public deliberation. Difficult issues have been addressed in online discussions and, sometimes at least, participants' positions change.

Listening to the City

In July 2002, the Civic Alliance to Rebuild Downtown New York, the Port Authority of New York and New Jersey, in association with non-profits Web Lab and America Speaks created Listening to the City Online Dialogues with a budget of $60,000. The dialogues focused on two things; plans for redevelopment of the World Trade Center site and the surrounding business district and neighborhoods of Lower Manhattan plus the creation of a permanent memorial for the victims and heroes of 9/11.

The dialogues took place in 26 small groups, all of which were active during the same two-week period. Messages could be posted to a group only by members assigned to that group. Participants could read and respond to each other's comments at any time, whether or not other members were online at the same time. The asynchronous system allowed members to join in when convenient and to spend time deliberately composing their responses. Half of the small groups were assigned an active facilitator and half were not.

During the two-week discussion, 808 participants working in 26 parallel discussion groups (half facilitated and half unfacilitated) posted more than 10,000 messages and responded to 32 polling questions largely based on themes that emerged during the dialogues.

Study of group demographics and relevant characteristics of the online participants revealed:

- nearly 9 percent of participants were family members of September 11 victims;
- more than 12 percent were survivors of the attack;
- almost 23 percent were employed in Lower Manhattan;
- 19 percent were residents of Lower Manhattan;

- nearly 13 percent were displaced or unemployed because of September 11;
- 44 percent of registrants were under 34 years old;
- nearly 25 percent of online participants were nonwhite.

(For more, see page 19 of the final report at: www.weblab. org/ltc/LTC_Report.pdf)

- A final poll among the 84 percent of participants who said they were satisfied with the dialogue indicated the chance to "have their say" and the mix of "people and perspectives" were the top reasons for their satisfaction.
- When asked, "Have your feelings or opinions about any of the issues discussed shifted as a result of these dialogues?" 55 percent of respondents said they had shifted.
- When asked whether their respect for people with whom they disagreed increased or decreased because of the dialogues, 53 percent said it had increased.[47]

Online deliberation works best when people have a chance to speak and be heard, express themselves and make decisions. This calls for sophisticated approaches to design and moderation, as well as close links between the explicit (and implicit) intentions of the deliberators who take part and institutional interest in taking the outcomes on board.

Complications and Obstacles

Three factors qualify some of the more hyperbolic claims about the Internet's potential as a public space:

1 the existence of a "digital divide" in terms of access and also literacy and skills;
2 the extent to which Internet use is characterized by public practices and modes of address, as opposed to private or personal interactions; and

3   the extent to which different contributions to public discourse
    on the Internet not only seek to address a public, but are able to com-
    mand public attention.

If the Internet has provided opportunities for many to participate in
public discourse, it has not provided them equally or for all. The digital
divide in Western democracies is diminishing, but not disappearing.
And, in global perspective, the picture is bleak indeed. In 2009, only
23 percent of the world's population had access to the Internet, with
Africa having the smallest level of Internet use per head of population
(5.6 percent).[48]

The digital divide is not just a question of access, but also, just as
importantly, of the uneven distribution of relevant literacy and keyboard
and computer skills. Even accepting Benkler's optimistic observation that
"computer literacy and skills, while far from universal, are much more
widely distributed than the skills and instruments of mass-media
production,"[49] the risk remains that the Internet might exacerbate and
reinforce existing inequalities, perhaps even giving rise to new ones.
If the Internet is significant in cultural, economic, and political terms,
we must also take account of Castells' claim that "exclusion from
these networks is one of the most damaging forms of exclusion in our
economy and in our culture."[50]

As well as user inequalities, which exclude some people from full
access to the Internet, there exist even greater asymmetries in relation
to the power to produce and disseminate online content. Some sites
and portals on the Internet are able to command a large amount of web
traffic and so maintain secure relations of public attention, plus healthy
and increasing advertising revenues. The danger here is that other
potential contributions to public discourse are being obscured and so
ignored by the same processes of media concentration and centralization that characterized the pre-Internet media and communications
environment. So, despite the impressive range of public communication
and information that is retrievable on the Internet in theory, in practice
the online media environment can look more like the old, mass media
where money is often a decisive factor in building and retaining
relations of public attention, and where a small number of media
institutions and organizations dominate the communications landscape. If there is a discernable trend on the web towards centralization
and concentration, there are very many countervailing tendencies. The

success of the highly interlinked blogosphere seems to enable the circulation of informal contributions to public discourse which have in the past been in some danger of being squeezed out. Even though certain sites command more public attention online, there are countless examples of cases where messages, information, and rumors emanating from seemingly humble origins have been disseminated widely and had a major impact. Benkler offers the sanguine conclusion that

> We now know that the network at all its various layers follows a degree of order, where some sites are vastly more visible then most. The order is loose enough, however, and exhibits a sufficient number of redundant paths from an enormous number of sites to another enormous number, that the effect is fundamentally different from the small number of commercial professional editors of the mass media.[51]

A second reason to be more sober about the Internet's contribution to publicness is uncertainty about the degree to which online communication contributes to public, as opposed to private or personal, discourse. Survey research suggests that most online interaction takes place within the private sphere: between individuals and impersonal computer content or between people who have already formed friendships. It is rare for people to go online to address or respond to citizens as a public. Dahlgren has observed that the Internet's use for political purposes "is clearly minor compared with other purposes to which it is put. The kinds of interaction taking place can only to a small degree be considered manifestations of the public sphere; democratic deliberation is completely overshadowed by consumerism, entertainment, non-political networking and chat, and so forth."[52] Of course, this depends upon how researchers define political communication. The tendency to confine civic publicness to such themes as election campaigning, deliberation about state policies, and the discussion of serious news, is too limited. What has traditionally been thought of as "the political" is increasingly discussed in terms that relate to broader areas of cultural life. The self-referential language and customs of traditional politics are giving way to new conceptions of the civic and political as taking place within the intimate spheres of personal experience. Power relationships are increasingly seen as taking place at the mundane, micro level of everyday experience. Daily struggles to be acknowledged, understood, and respected, whether in the home, the workplace, the playground, or the pub, are increasingly recognized as political. People who do not think of themselves as acting politically frequently find themselves employing democratic discourses and principles in order to pursue what they might prefer to think of as personal campaigns for a better life. As we shall argue in the next chapter, unless conceptions of publicness and the political are liberated from those which currently dominate the atmosphere of the public sphere, both terms will come to be regarded as increasingly marginal to the lifeworlds of most people.

A rather different version of the argument that online communication narrows and fragments public debate is put by theorists who claim that, whereas mainstream media institutions have typically helped to moderate the problem of group polarization by simplifying available information choices and retaining control over content, the Internet might contributes to a decline in centripetal communication and an increase in centrifugal communication. From this perspective, media abundance and increased choice may mean that very many individuals, from their "little private worlds" in front of the screen, are able to avoid encountering significant public differences of identity, interest, and perspective, and, perhaps, can escape from the world and avoid connecting with public concerns. Sunstein[53] offers a well-known critique of the Internet's "fragmenting" effects. Given the increase in personal choice and control over information, the Internet may allow us to restrict our experiences only to encounters with "like-minded" others. So despite the diversity of identities, interest, or perspective represented or made present on the Internet in theory, users may, in practice, seek out information and interactions that only reflect back and reinforce prior attachments and identification. Group differences are then balkanized and reinforced, rather than openly critiqued, and opportunities for the production of common shared public realities are diminished. As Calhoun puts it,

> What computer-mediated communication adds is a greater capacity to avoid public interaction of the kind that would pull one beyond one's immediate personal choices of taste and culture . . . New technologies often enhance "categorical" identities rather than the dense and multiplex webs of interpersonal relationships the label "network" suggests and that we commonly associate with the idea of community . . .[54]

Sunstein argues that "for all their problems, and their unmistakable limitations and biases" the mainstream media have performed some important democratic functions. For example,

People who rely on such intermediaries have a range of chance encounters, involving shared experience with diverse others, and also exposure to material that they did not specifically choose. You might, for example, read the city newspaper, and in the process come across stories that you would not have selected if you had the power to control what you see.[55]

According to this critique, the very pluralizing and personalizing features that appear to make the Internet more individually meaningful may well contribute to collective impoverishment.

Thirdly, the ability to speak through the media and address others is only democratically significant if there is a possibility of being seen and heard. The ability to attain visibility and secure and command relatively stable relations of public attention across time and space are not equally distributed opportunities. Contrary to the claims of the Declaration of the Independence of Cyberspace, communicative power online is determined by money, reputation, and organizational resources. While it is true that almost anyone can start their own blog, it is equally true that most blogs are never read by more people than the blogger would be likely to encounter in her local pub, and the few blogs that do reach millions of people are generally supported by marketing and publicity machines that few people could ever afford to employ. In a sophisticated network analysis of the blogosphere, Drezner and Farrell argue that, despite the volume of bloggers, estimated at around 10 million, and the volume of news posts, their influence is not commensurate with their productivity since the distribution of weblinks and the orientatioin of traffic is skewed so that a few bloggers actually receive a disproportionate amount of attention.[56] Blog producers and readers who are not major media organizations, Internet service providers, or mainstream political parties are faced with a frustrating coordination problem:

Most bloggers wish to maximize their readership, but face very substantial difficulties in gaining new readers. Given the vast number of blogs even in the political subsection of the blogosphere, it is extraordinarily hard for them to attract readers, even when they have something interesting and unique to offer. Blog readers, for their part, want to find interesting blog posts – in terms of either new information or a compelling interpretation of old information. However, given search costs and limited time, it is nearly impossible for readers to sift through the vast amounts of available material in order to find the interesting posts.[57]

In order for smaller blogs to gain attention, they must seek to link to and filtered by the few larger blogs which act as new-media gate-keepers to the virtual public sphere. There are blogs – as well as websites, email lists and other online spaces – that manage to reach a much larger readership than one would expect from their limited resource base, but these are exceptions. Generally speaking, gaining attention online is skewed towards the economically and politically powerful, although there is some evidence to suggest that smaller players have more chance of setting an agenda online than offline.

A Reconfigured Media Ecology

Even the most sceptical observer of new media developments is bound to accept that the emergence of the Internet has reconfigured the information and communication environment. Like broadcasting in the early twentieth century and the printing press 500 years earlier, the Internet has brought about new ways of producing, acquiring, sharing, and challenging what people need to know. It has changed the ways in which older media are used. It has reshaped wider social relations, often having unintended consequences for key social activities such as working, learning, travelling, purchasing goods, making friends, and being governed. The Internet has not displaced traditional media and will probably never do so, but it has reconfigured the ecology of public information and communication.

Too often this reconfiguration is spoken and written about in natur-alistic terms, as if digital media are some sort of Darwinian mutation forcing themselves upon us with an implacable evolutionary vigor. Even the hyperbolic proclamations quoted at the beginning of this chapter, while seeming to grant renewed and stupendous powers of agency to the public, imply that this is somehow driven by an irresistible force of technology. But, like every other technology, these media are made, not inherited. As Orlikowski has rightly stated regarding the social shaping of technologies,

Technology is physically constructed by actors working within a given social context, and technology is socially constructed by actors through the different meanings they attach to it and the various features they emphasize and use. However, it is also the case that once developed and deployed, technology tends to become reified and institutionalized, losing its connection with the human agents that constructed it or gave it meaning, and it appears to be part of the objective, structural properties of the organization.[58]

This process of cultural reification has particular relevance to the relationship between digital media and democratic publicness, for it raises a key question about the extent to which technologies designed and developed for sale and profit can be utilized as tools of public empowerment. The governance of the Internet, which is currently a messy compromise between private audacity and public bureaucracy, is a product of history rather than inevitability. Just as broadcasting in the 1920s was regarded in some countries as a space of inviolable free enterprise and in others as the locus for a public cultural service, there are choices to be made about who and what we want the Internet to serve. Much energy is currently dedicated to eradicating "harmful" online content (ranging from child pornography to unwanted expressions of opinion in countries ruled by dictatorships), but very little effort has gone into attempts to create sites and circuits of public discussion that bring citizens closer to the levers of policy-forming and decision-making power. Attempts to set out a public service function for the Internet, as pursued in recent years, have all been frustrated by two political obstacles. The first is genuine uncertainty on the part of policy-makers, media producers, and technologists about what a democratic mediaspace would look like. Sennett's observation that "were modern architects asked to design spaces that better promote democracy, they would lay down their pens; there is no modern design equivalent to the ancient assembly"[59] well captures the prevailing sense of technical and aesthetic reticence to think both imaginatively and practically about public empowerment. The tendency has been to fall back upon tired rhetorical simulations of democracy ("Have Your Say" and "Your Shout" message boards), gimmicks offering connection without efficacy (the Ten Downing Street e-petitions come to mind), or digital replications of traditional offline practices (such as e-voting.) As the examples given in this chapter demonstrate, there are lots of ways in which people are using the Internet to challenge officialdom, protest, debate, network, produce common meanings, and make their presence felt, but these spaces of democracy are largely disconnected from the old institutions of representation which go on as if this intensifying subterranean buzz can be ignored or patronized. There is a need for imaginative institution-building with a view to connecting the energy, experience, and heterogeneity of online – and offline – voices to the debates, decisions, and reflections of governance at every level.

A second frustration facing efforts to think about the reconfigured media ecology as a public space emanates from growing uncertainties about who or what constitutes the public. As we shall discuss in the next chapter, it is much easier to imagine the public as an audience "somewhere out there," awaiting its next supply of entertainment or news, than as the complex entity that is forever spoken for and addressed, but rarely witnessed on its own terms.

6

Fractured Publics, Contested Publicness

Definitions of the public interest that once appeared to be clear and immutable seem in recent times to have become fragile and in need of reconceptualization. The public, as an historical actor, has come to be seen as a fractured and fragmented entity, splintered by debates about identity, belonging, and responsibility. As the idea of a singular, potentially univocal public is abandoned, a pluralistic conception of the public as a patchwork of co-existing and overlapping communities has emerged. This fractured public lacks the metaphysical integrity that once gave legitimacy to notions of sovereign nationhood and moral universalism.

The socio-spatial boundaries between publicness and privacy are similarly blurred. Boundaries between public and private have become increasingly unstable and bedevilled by ambiguities between the intimate and the impersonal, the private and the performative, the consumerist and the civic dimensions of everyday life. As Morrison et al. have shown, until recently privacy has tended to be regarded by liberal theorists as "a moral or human right" associated with what it means to be "an autonomous human being."[1] As a right, privacy has been most commonly cherished in the context of familial, financial, and sexual information about ourselves that we do not wish to share with others. But in a society dominated (negatively) by surveillance cameras, government databases, and leaky telephone and email exchanges, and (more popularly) by porous social networks such as Facebook, Youtube, and MySpace, by user-generated media content, and by reality TV shows specializing in the maximum exposure of personal interaction, it is no longer obvious when one is entering or leaving the attendant gaze of the public domain.

At the same time, institutions and events that once seemed to be inherently public and civic – schools, railways, broadcasting, high streets, and roads – are being privatized, forcing traditional acts of public engagement into spaces designed for unaccountable private gain. Can a privately run shopping mall, with its own laws and security guards, any longer be described as a public space? Are privately funded academies free to raise critical questions about the corporate (ir)responsibility of their sponsors? Can an online public sphere develop within an environment dominated by proprietorial software and the constraints of intellectual copyright? The uncertainties posed by these questions undermine the ontological foundations of publicness. If any meaning is to be attached to this term, a more flexible and nuanced language is required.

Given the instability and ambiguity of the public and publicness in the contemporary lexicon, to speak of a *public interest*, be it local, national, or global, has become deeply problematic. Historically, the notion of a public interest derived from the belief that there are ways of arranging socio-cultural affairs that can benefit all rather than some. Examples of such universal benefits include services such as street cleaning, traffic lights, and the provision of free public libraries. In the context of the media, there are two ways of conceiving this public interest. The first is to think of the public as an entity that must be engendered, cultivated, and protected through the promotion of specific values. When critics accuse the BBC of being dominated by "anti-British propaganda" or a "left-liberal bias," they are expressing anxiety that the UK's public service broadcaster is failing to play its role in creating, promoting, and sustaining a particular kind of public. To speak of the public interest in this way assumes the existence of an essentialist script of appropriate civic norms. A second way to think of the public interest is in terms of plurality and ongoing contestation. In this sense, addressing or promoting the public interest entails a disposition which regards the public interest as a moot entity that cannot and should not be essentialized.

The philosopher Richard Rorty has distinguished between two radically different approaches to understanding the world. The first employs what he calls a "final vocabulary" with a view to capturing the metaphysical essence of social reality. "The metaphysician," argues

Rorty, is "attached to common sense, in that he does not question the platitudes which encapsulate the use of a given final vocabulary, and in particular the platitude which says there is a single permanent reality to be found behind the many temporary appearances."[2] In contrast to this is the ironic perspective, which assumes that all social phenomena and values, however established and firmly defined, are open to being described in new ways which can be played off against the old; that everything around us is open to redescription because nothing is ever historically complete. Ironists, according to Rorty, are "never quite able to take themselves seriously" because they are "always aware that the terms in which they describe themselves are subject to change, always aware of the contingency and fragility of their final vocabularies, and thus of their selves."[3] The contrast between these two perspectives upon reality – the metaphysical and the ironic – provides a useful framework for thinking about the uncertainties and ambiguities surrounding contemporary notions of the public interest. For metaphysical thinkers, the public interest must be defined and delimited with a view to drawing clear lines, both between members and non-members of the public, and between events, relationships, and issues which belong in the public sphere and those which do not. In contrast, ironists are relaxed about the kind of blurred boundaries we have been discussing above. They regard the public (as actor and as space) as a fluid domain, expanding and contracting in response to political, cultural, and economic pressures. Ironists do not regard membership of a public as a permanent commitment calling for a special kind of loyalty, but imagine themselves having a range of attachments to publics, some more intense and demanding than others. Neither are ironists much troubled by shifting boundaries between public and private aspects of life or areas of society, for they tend to see such boundaries as a consequence of negotiation and redescription rather than as mutually exclusive and inviolable zones.

While Rorty's insight into the competing languages and tones of social reality is extremely valuable, his writings are surprisingly silent on the question of how these perspectives are produced and circulated. Rorty presents his argument as if each individual arrives at metaphysical or ironic positions through a process of personal introspection. In fact, the ways in which people come to describe and redescribe social reality is highly influenced by knowledge-producing institutions, foremost amongst which are schools, religious organizations, and the media. The extent to which the media are dominated by a final vocabulary (of the sort adopted in the oppressively confident tones of early British and American broadcasting) or an ironic register (typified by the eclecticism of the contemporary liberal media's loose boundaries between news and entertainment, fact and satire, drama and record) will play a significant role in determining the terms of public discourse – and of discourse about what constitutes the public interest.

Media organizations in which a final vocabulary prevails would seek above all else to transmit truth – indeed, the Truth – to their audiences. Following the injunction of John Reith, the first Director-General of the BBC, they would aim to serve the public by informing it of a range of facts, insights, and values that it might not stumble upon on its own. They would endeavor to instil in the audience not only a final vocabulary that would frame "correct thinking," but proper ways of expressing that vocabulary: Received Pronunciation and the censorship of vulgarity. For much of their early history, mainstream British and American media organizations adopted precisely such a stance, often opening them to the accusation of being arrogant, condescending, and illiberal. In more recent times, the media have tended to be characterized by a more ironic perspective: they are reluctant to suggest that truths are fully known, narratives ever complete, or values absolute. Some critics accuse the contemporary media of being timidly relativist, lacking core moral values, and irresponsibly pandering to popular whims. But such is the price of perpetual redescription; for if liberalism rather than fundamentalism is to prevail, all knowledge, and the foundations of producing and accessing it, must be open to question. Nothing is permanently settled. The jury is forever deliberating.

Early twentieth-century broadcasters, especially those committed to a public service ethos, saw their task as being to define the public as a singular, inclusive, and quantifiable object of address; to become *the* public sphere of national discourse; and to police the boundaries of appropriate public conduct. This grand project could not avoid delineating the ambit of the public in ideological terms, as well as excluding from the public terrain all kinds of social actors who believed they had a right to be there. In more recent times this constraining representation of the public has become unsustainable. As Silverstone has suggested,

> For generations . . . we could avoid, disguise or deny such plurality. Our everyday lives were not necessarily lived in ways that forced the issue, at least on a scale beyond the face-to-face of village or community. But

now they are. The mediated globe involves lifting the veil on difference. It cannot be avoided. It is seen and heard daily.[4]

In making difference more conspicuous, contemporary media technologies, techniques, and values undermine the illusion of a finally describable, homogeneous public and give rise to new questions about how diverse (and sometimes mutually antagonistic) publics can be introduced to one another; how they can be encouraged to witness themselves critically and reflectively, and how vast, differentiated societies can arrive at common responses to complex problems. Whereas early media producers endeavored to maintain social order, improve moral standards, and inform political opinion *on behalf of* a seemingly identifiable public, contemporary media producers eschew such universalist ambitions, operating instead within and across the fragmented identities of pluralistic publics.

The contrast between the BBC's articulated objectives in the early twentieth and twenty-first centuries well illustrates these radically different conceptions of the public interest. For Reith, the BBC's task was to create a "unity of the nervous system of the body politic" by becoming "the integrator for democracy."[5] Conceived as a process of integration, democracy could only ever have limited tolerance for cultural dissent. In a 1925 memorandum setting out the objectives of the new corporation, Reith argued that a positive effect of public broadcasting would be to make "the nation as one man."[6] Never was this commitment to national integration more vigorously pursued than during the 1926 General Strike, when Reith infamously argued that "since the BBC was a national institution, and since the Government in this crisis were acting for the people . . . the BBC was for the Government in this crisis too."[7] This paternalistic synthesis between socio-cultural integration and political propaganda remained the dominant perspective of early British public service broadcasting, whether in its coverage of parliamentary debates or its production of soap operas, such as *The Archers*, which was originally devised as a propaganda vehicle for the Ministry of Agriculture.

Eighty years later, the BBC stated its contribution to the creation of national value in conspicuously pluralistic terms. *Building Public Value* contains no fewer than 136 references to "community" and one of the five key objectives set out for the twenty-first-century BBC was to nurture "social and community value": "By enabling the UK's many communities to see what they hold in common and how they differ, the BBC seeks to build social cohesion and tolerance through greater understanding."[8] The extent of the BBC's wish to transcend the "nation as one man" principle can be sensed from its explicit commitments to:

> foster greater audience understanding of cultural differences across the UK population, in ethnicity, faith, sexuality, ability/disability and age; show particular sensitivity in reporting issues and events which may be socially divisive . . . faithfully reflect modern Britain's diversity in mainstream as well as specialist programmes; set new targets for the on-air portrayal of ethnic minorities, those with disabilities and those from other minorities; monitor usage of, and attitudes to, the BBC by the UK's minorities, listen to their concerns and priorities, and reflect those concerns in the future development of services.[9]

To what extent are these realistic aspirations? How far can the media become truly accountable to the public? Can ways be found to acknowledge the presence of diverse publics within the contemporary mediascape? If a more pluralistic media is achievable, can this be compatible with a public sphere in which, on some occasions at least, the diverse strands and strata of society come together in common discourse? And, if such collective publicness is desirable and feasible, what hope is there that it might give rise to more than an animated talking shop? In short, to what extent might media publics have a meaningful impact upon political outcomes? These pressing questions of policy and practice go beyond traditional, liberal aspirations for media to be characterized by honesty, fairness, and critical reason. While such goals remain indispensable benchmarks of a democratic media system, and continue to demand organizational, ethical, and economic support to sustain and develop them, they fail to address the more fragmented, variegated landscape of contemporary citizenship.

In abandoning the convenient illusion of a singular public inhabiting a central discursive sphere, the media are faced with four key challenges:

1 to provide tools, skills, and content that will allow publics to witness themselves and their lifeworlds;
2 to provide tools, skills, and content that will help diverse publics to make sense of one another;
3 to monitor, facilitate, and connect public deliberation on matters of common interest and concern;

4   to provide tools, skills, and content that will enable citizens to understanding the multifaceted and often discreet workings of power, and to hold the powerful to account in ways that can make a difference.

These challenges seem to be incompatible with the notion of a finally describable public interest. Only by adopting the ironist's perspective of regarding the public in historicist rather than essentialist terms are these objectives likely to escape the pitfalls of piety and tokenism. In the following sections, we explore these challenges in some detail, with a view to making some tentative proposals for the future of public service communication in societies that describe themselves as democratic.

Meeting Ourselves

Human beings, as social animals, have a need to be acknowledged. At a personal level, acknowledgment arises from specific knowledge: one is liked, loathed, feared, ridiculed, trusted, admired, imitated, remembered, addressed, insulted, desired because of who one is – or appears to be. Forming connections, cultivating identities, and dealing with intimate disappointments is a complex and time-consuming part of daily inter-personal communication. It is the most common subject of discussion between people and, for most of us, the ongoing drama of our personal relationships, which few others would comprehend or care about, is the most important matter in our lives. Culture, in other words, is rooted in the mundane experience of being and performing ourselves in the presence of others.

The work of representing and making sense of private lifeworlds has traditionally been undertaken by writers and artists rather than the press and politicians. While the dramas and deliberations of the public sphere are represented in the language of official politics, the nuanced realities of everyday experience are acted out in plays and films, depicted visually in paintings and photographs, and narrated in novels. The French realist novel of the nineteenth century played a particularly important and original role in opening up the private sphere to public inspection. The character of this genre was well expressed by Raymond Williams:

> When I think of the realist tradition in fiction, I think of the kind of novel which creates and judges the quality of a whole way of life in terms of the qualities of persons. The balance involved in this achievement is perhaps the most important thing about it . . . the distinction of this kind is that it offers a valuing of a whole way of life, a society that is larger than any of the individuals composing it, and at the same time valuing creations of human beings who, while belonging to and affected by and helping to define this way of life, are also, in their own terms, ends in themselves . . . We attend with our whole senses to every aspect of the general life, yet the centre of value is always in the individual human person – not any one isolated person, but the many persons who are the reality of the general life.[10]

This dialectical interaction between the social and the personal is at the heart of the realist project in artistic representation and raises significant challenges for any creative producer attempting to depict the public. For, as Williams understood and writers like Zola, Eliot, and Gissing were constantly exploring, realism is always in danger of becoming unbalanced: of depicting the individual member of the public either as a mere instrument of social control or as a romantic protagonist capable of carving out a personal existence beyond or beneath the social. The great works of realist literature were those that introduced the public and its particular members in terms that reflected the ways in which mundane experience is generated through a dynamic mix of social determinism and personal agency.

Critics of the realist writers baulked at their emphasis upon "the unpleasant, the exposed [and] the sordid"[11] aspects of everyday reality and their tendency to ignore the social contexts and constraints which limited the reality of "ordinary" people. In fact, both criticisms stemmed from the same suspicion: that realist writers were somehow entering the world of the "ordinary" as bourgeois tourists and reporters, bringing back to their sensitive readers horrific accounts of the mass public, while protecting their readers from concerns about the iniquities of the social order. When George Eliot claimed (in *Adam Bede*) to be holding up a mirror to social reality, she, like other realist writers, exposed herself to the accusation of providing a merely selective account, intended to reinforce her readers' beliefs about the limited moral and intellectual capacity of ordinary people, while failing to explore fully the social (and particularly economic) constraints placed upon them. Nonetheless, realist writers were anxious to claim that their novels were for the first time giving exposure to the lives of hitherto neglected common people; that they were offering a form of literary enfranchizement yet to be granted within the political sphere. Auerbach, in his magisterial history of literary realism, quotes Edmond and Jules Goncourt's preface to their 1864 novel, *Germinie Lacerteux*:

> Living in the nineteenth century, in a time of universal suffrage, of democracy, of liberalism, we asked ourselves if what is called "the lower classes" did not have a right to the Novel; if that world beneath a world, the people, must remain under the literary interdict and disdain of authors who have so far kept silent upon the soul and the heart which it may have. We asked ourselves if, for the writer and the reader, there were still, in these years of equality in which we live, unworthy classes, troubles too base, dramas too foul-mouthed, catastrophes too little noble in their terror.[12]

This passage embodies both the strengths and weaknesses of literary realism. The authors clearly see their novel as performing a democratic function by introducing readers to the world of the *demos*, but this is achieved by a process of descent into a reality that can only ever reveal sordid insights. (Much the same assumption was to influence British kitchen-sink drama in the late 1950s, and the subsequent British – though not American – television soap-opera tradition.) Obsessed by the domestic duplicity, cultural vulgarity, and routine criminality of city dwellers, a realist tradition running from Gissing's *Nether World* through Orwell's *Down and Out in Paris and London* to the BBC soap opera, *EastEnders*, has contributed to a bleak narrative of everyday life.

While literary and cinematic realism has been limited by the need to construct rhetorically the objects that they claim to be representing, early twentieth-century documentary-makers saw themselves as being capable of overcoming this limitation by focusing on the faithful depiction of actuality. This phenomenological conceit depends upon an assumed contradistinction between fiction, which "harbors echoes of dreams and daydreams, sharing structures of fantasy with them" and documentary which "mimics the canons of expository argument, the making of a case, and the call to public rather than private response."[13] Early documentarists such as Grierson and Jennings seemed to believe that the inherent publicness of their referents diminished the scope for rhetorical constructions that were at odds with everyday experience.

Although, as we shall show, these directors were not naïvely committed to the mimetic reproduction of reality, they saw the value of the images they produced as being accountable to a public which could, in a certain democratic sense, determine their veracity. This amounted to more than endeavoring to provide a credible picture of life as it is lived; following Williams' counsel to capture "a whole way of life," in which the personal and social are dialectically interrelated, documentary realists set out to produce an aesthetically convincing contextualized account of "the many persons who are the reality of the general life."[14]

But, as with other seemingly indexical versions of realistic art, such as photography, documentary production is inevitably encoded, framed, focused, and arranged. As Grierson himself put it, "documentary proper" not only describes "natural material," but arranges, rearranges, and creatively shapes it.[15] This "creative treatment of actuality" is a process of aesthetic redescription which subjects social reality to an ironic gaze: a form of scrutiny which renders it all the more authentic for its ambiguity.

In this sense, reality TV formats, such as *Big Brother*, which have been derided as "the depths of exploitation and voyeurism, cruelty and exploitation"[16] can be seen as contributing to the project of realist redescription. As Corner notes, "right at the heart of the series is the idea of observing what is a mode of 'real' behavior," even though "the material and temporal conditions for that behavior have been entirely constructed by television itself."[17] Unlike earlier documentary forms which sought to focus upon the significance of the social world, *Big Brother* attends to microsocial relationships, often overlooked in accounts of the big picture, not least because they are often discrete and rhizomatic in their structure. Such everyday experience is grounded in the sensibility of the body and its messy encounters with other bodies within shared spaces of both mental and physical habitation. In *Big Brother* there is an implicit inseparability of mind and body, private and public, individual and social. According to Corner, the program "dispenses with the difficulties of extracting the personal from the social" by

> building its own social precisely for the purpose of revealing the personal. This social is *comprehensively available* to television, it has indeed been built for the daily delivery of behavior to camera. Strictly speaking, then, the circumstances are not so much those of observation as those of *display*; living space is also performance space.[18]

But is not all living space to some extent a performance space, and might not one important function of television as public witness be to allow us to observe and interrogate the integrity and credibility of one another's social performances? Might, indeed, one of the most revealing tasks of realism be to set the stage and terms for mutual acknowledgment and judgment? If so, then far from being a distraction from matters of public interest (such as news and current affairs), surveillant media formats that enable the public to describe and redscribe itself may well provide the kind of socio-psychological insights that films about coal miners, postal deliveries, and fishermen provided in a more one-sided manner in the 1930s. Specifically, more recent formats have added three elements to the realist mix that could at least contribute to democratic value:

1   a focus upon the mundane experiences, pleasures, challenges, instabilities, and uncertainties of hitherto neglected individuals, for example, children, the bereaved, transsexuals, criminals, aristocrats, police officers, prisoners, the terminally ill, eccentrics, and lottery winners (to name but a random sample of recent reality TV subjects);
2   an opportunity to observe people over long periods of time (*7-Up*),[19] providing a longitudinal opportunity to explore interactions between personal and social developments, and with limited temporal interruption, through streaming (*Big Brother*), allowing the viewer unprecedented control over the surveillant gaze;
3   the use of interactive communication technologies for voting on reactions to personal behavior and, as importantly, to form communities of discussion reflecting upon, and potentially intervening in, what is being witnessed.

If media interactivity can make teaching and learning more effective, commerce more convenient to conduct, public information more accessible? and friendships easier to maintain, surely it can also enable publics to make their presence felt in ways that can make a difference.

Encountering the Other

In its various forms and guises, media realism discloses and exposes us to ourselves, often stretching the first person plural to embrace the unfamiliar and enigmatic. Realism operates along an ontological spectrum, exploring a broad range of differences and representing them as somehow related to one another, as if revealing primordial connections. From this realist perspective, *terra incognita* is regarded as an imaginative failure, a relationship not yet acknowledged or explained. But what of those realities that are beyond acknowledgment or common comprehension: that seem to be inconceivable, inexpressible, and alien? We are not speaking here about censorship (although it certainly takes place), but a particular kind of sensibility, dominating most mainstream media production, which privileges the subjective feelings of "people like us" and delicately excludes, marginalizes, or renders insignificant that which challenges our sense of ourselves as familiar beings. As Chouliaraki suggests, the media "are almost obsessively preoccupied with our 'interiorities' – our intimate relationships, fears and desires, homes, bodies, and appearance."[20] As narratives are sucked inwards, towards the nation, the community, and, above all, the self, social reality comes to have meaning only in terms of affective correspondence. Recognition becomes the sole legitimacy for the real. Chouliaraki argues that "the news genre, formal and detached from emotion as it often appears to be, becomes part of this culture of intimacy, in so far as it, implicitly, reserves the potential for us to pity 'our' own suffering and leaves the far away 'other' outside our horizon of care and responsibility."[21]

The philosopher Emannuel Lévinas offers a useful way of thinking about this failure of responsibility to the "other." In his distinction between the *Dit* (Said) and *Dire* (Saying) of everyday speech, he argues that what is *Said* comprises the routine transmission and reception of messages, while *Saying* refers to the way in which the recipient of communication is approached and addressed. The Saying is "an ethical event," insofar as it conveys the speaker's sense of proximity to the addressed. For example, the Saying of a media report about public opinion on a particular issue will signify all kinds of assumptions, exclusions, and reservations about who constitutes the public and how trustworthy its opinion is likely to be, well before the act of describing the opinion in question even begins. The Saying is a tone or manner that determines the reading of what is Said. This rather complicated distinction is helpful in calling into question not only what the media say, but how it is said. In media references to the public – and especially those parts of the public which exist on the peripheries of mainstream media experience – misunderstanding is less likely to arise from censorship or intentional distortion than from forms of linguistic and semiotic distancing which imply that certain people are best thought of as "they," which allow message receivers to feel well removed from the experience or consequences of others' suffering which can be silently relegated to the category of the socially extraneous.

While Section 264(4)(i) of the UK's Communications Act (2003) states that public service broadcasters must "reflect the lives and concerns of different communities and cultural interests and traditions within the UK" and the broadcasting regulator, Ofcom, has published a review of public service broadcasting identifying one of its four objectives as being "to support a tolerant and inclusive society, through programs which reflect the lives of different people and communities within the UK, encourage a better understanding of different cultures and, on occasion, bring the nation together for shared experiences,"[22] many groups within British society feel under-represented by the media, not simply in terms of being excluded. British Muslims, for example, feel that, while frequently reported in the press and on television, they are the victims of a highly strereotypical image. Ahmed argues that "The traditional Orientalist stereotypes of Muslims as political anarchists and tyrants at home subjugating their women have been disseminated in the media as caricatures and stereotypes."[23] The conflation of the terms "Muslim" and "terrorist" has almost become a default position in some British newspapers. Writing about the Canadian press after 9/11, Elmasry noted that "the frequent demonic portrayal of Islam and Muslims has been one of the most persistent, virulent and socially significant sources of anti-Islam."[24] Persistent stereotypes of Muslims as "other than us" are supported by deep layers of Orientalist ideology which, through films and novels as well as news and documentaries, has identified the West as symbolically secure, civilized, and trustworthy, in contrast to the cultures of potentially intrusive outsiders.

Otherness is not confined to the geographically distant and culturally exotic. There are countless domestic spaces and acts of otherness that the mainstream media seem reluctant or unable to reflect within their representations of social reality. For example, municipal housing estates (public housing) rarely feature in the British media except as backdrops for stories about street crime. And yet one fifth of the British population live on these estates, engaging in a variety of daily experiences that do not revolve around the fear or consequences of crime. Few media producers live in these spaces and are only likely to enter them in search of a narrow range of images reflecting social inadequacy and breakdown. Even soaps, in their relentless quest for imagined community, steer clear of municipal housing estates, preferring to set their accounts of "everyday life" within romanticized, obsolete environments: the market square of *EastEnders*; the terraced houses of *Coronation Street*; the rural parish of *Emmerdale.* A consequence of making certain spaces invisible within the media is to circumscribe their public value; to cast a shadow upon their publicness by making them seem strange.

Whole areas of human activity fall victim to these mediated constructions of otherness. For example, although television viewers and newspaper readers typically spend most of their days "at work," they read or see little about their workplaces in the media's representation of social reality. The TV program *The Office* provided a rare, albeit comedic, glimpse into the vapidly ritualized and hierarchically structured world of the post-industrial workplace, but the act of working, in all of its diversely creative forms (which was of such interest to the early documentary-makers), is rarely the focus of contemporary media production. Instead, working time is represented as the other to free, observable, and stimulating leisure time. The workplace, alongside the street, is the most common space of public interaction, within which the frustrations, negotiations, protocols, and pleasures of being thrown together with others are most vividly experienced. But media accounts of workplaces tend to provide narrow and highly personalized representations of working life: narrow because they generally focus upon the dramatization of relatively atypical work environments, such as hospitals, police stations, or small work units; and personalized in their emphasis upon the workplace as a site of emotional community rather than corporate control.

Media organizations have been challenged to be more culturally pluralistic.[25] This is not simply a matter of showing more black faces on prime-time programs, but of reflecting the diverse composition of society at every level of media production. A representative of PACT, the independent media producers' organization, is reported by Sreberny as stating that "You look at telly and you see Trevor McDonald and other people on Channel 4 news and get the idea that it's all mixed up, and it really isn't. It's not like that behind the cameras at all."[26] Former BBC Director-General, Greg Dyke, accused the corporation of being "hideously white" and one of its most highly paid celebrity presenters, Jonathan Ross, has said that "Most of the guys you see here are working on the door, carrying a cloth or cleaning up."[27] These concerns are supported by figures: despite the fact that ethnic minority staff made up 11 percent of the BBC workforce in 2007, fewer than 2 percent were in senior management positions and 75 percent were in the lowest-paid category of employees. Clearly, there is scope for institutional change, to reflect not only the ethnic make-up of the society that the BBC is charged to reflect, but also those socio-economic groups beyond the metropolitan middle class.

But in an age of global information flows, time-space compression, and borderless communication networks, representing the other cannot simply be a matter of enhancing institutional heterogeneity. For media organizations to serve as translators and facilitators of understanding and respect *between and within* publics, change needs to be dispositional as well as institutional. A cosmopolitan sensibility towards the mediation of a world that is both inescapably interconnected and culturally fragmented is the only likely basis upon which the media can meet the ethical challenge of bridging (or, at the very least, identifying) the distances between diverse publics. The core of this cosmopolitan sensibility involves a repositioning of the media, eschewing exclusive attachments to particular places, histories, or publics. In place of an imagined universal addressee occupying a singular public sphere, cosmopolitan public communication entails a sense of being open to the world and its diverse modes of experience. As Turner has put it, in outlining his argument for "cosmopolitan irony," "scepticism and distance from one's own tradition are the basis of an obligation of care and stewardship for other cultures."[28] This does not call for a dissolution of existing cultural attachments and connections, but a sensitivity to what is beyond them. Rorty's contrast between the language of metaphysical essentialism and ironic redescription is at the heart of this dispositional challenge. From a metaphysical perspective, globalization tends to be depicted as an unfolding of inevitable economic reality. The function of the media in this context is to describe global trends as if they were natural; to serve as a cultural shock absorber as settled meanings and beliefs are destabilized. The ironic/redescriptive approach to the global reflects the fluidity of contemporary identities, the delicate interactions between the local and the worldly, and the new challenges to collective action, not as if they are or ever could be settled patterns, but as undetermined cultural mutations. In short, the ironic perspective calls for an ethical position that rejects the idea of a fixed and singular "us"; that extends the communicative possibilities of "we-ness."

There were discernible signs in the 1990s of a move towards broader, more ironically questioning media perspectives upon questions of place, identity, and values, but such redscriptive confidence was shattered by the events of 9/11 and the subsequent "war on terror." The mainstream media mood post-9/11 has been dominated by a Manichaean contrast between "us" and "them": a mainly white, Euro-American, Judeo-Christian public and its subversive, disruptive other. What Silverstone has described as a "rhetoric of evil" has infiltrated the mainstream media, most manifestly in the United States, but also elsewhere, dragging public discourse back to a vocabulary that seemed to have been relinquished with the ascendancy of the Enlightenment. As Silverstone puts it,

> Evil is becoming, once again, a taken-for-granted category of analysis and judgment, particularly in the post-9/11 world. The problem comes when the notion of evil is seen as sufficient explanation for those wrongs, and worse, as a justification for action. The paradox is, of course . . . that in a world in which evil is believed to be only a property of the other, it is almost inevitable that such an imposition will rebound. Those who call it become it. Evil has the potential to be perniciously double-edged.[29]

Of course, this paradox is not entirely new. In the 1980s the Reagan administration labeled the Soviet bloc as an "evil empire" because of its lack of democracy, but after the fall of the Berlin Wall the West's own democratic claims were critically scrutinized by commentators who saw within it significant gaps between self-description and reality. The US president spoke after 9/11 of a "crusade" against alien values, thereby evoking memories of the Christian history of fundamentalist militancy. Rhetorics of evil, with their implication that the other need not be addressed as they are irrevocably outside, contribute to a form of cultural sclerosis in which publicness is principally defined by exclusion. For the media to serve the public at all effectively and democratically, it must be consciously committed to precisely the opposite end: to defining publicness in terms of promiscuous inclusion.

Facilitating Public Deliberation

Enabling people to recognize themselves and acknowledge others is a necessary but not sufficient prerequisite for the media to work in the public interest. Beyond these monitorial relationships of mutual recognition and accountability, the public must be able to question its own values, attitudes, and opinions; to reflect upon its desires, fears, plans, and projections with an openness to changing perspectives. This process of public self-reflection is known as deliberation. By deliberating with one another, citizens can go beyond the promotion of established interests and preferences, taking up new positions in response to convincing argument, evidence, and anecdote.

As we have shown in chapter 3, the mainstream media provide rare and limited opportunities for members of the public to deliberate freely upon the wide range of issues that affect them. Most mediated discussion is managed and edited in ways that leave active citizens with something to say feeling like outsiders trespassing upon the sanctity of official communication spaces. There are opportunities to "listen in" to deliberations conducted within the confines of studios or parliamentary chambers, but democratic political discussion entails more than the chance to attend to the voices of remote others. Just as in the eighteenth century there was an elitist notion of *virtual representation* which justified the right of property-owners to vote on behalf of the property-less majority, so we have a contemporary practice of *virtual deliberation*, which allows high-profile, well-educated and confident people to discuss political and social issues on behalf of the spectating audience. Although there is no shortage of phone-ins, studio-audience discussions and online fora to which people are invited to contribute their views, these rarely take a deliberative form. On the contrary, public participation in the media is all too often reduced to a series of 20-second snapshot comments, cut off before anything resembling deliberation could possibly take shape.

Democratic deliberation, whether on a local, national, or global scale, can only take place if certain conditions are met. Firstly, it must be open to all to set the agenda, take part in discussion, and determine the outcome, independently of unequal resources and interests. Secondly, there must be an opportunity for all views to be expressed openly, regardless of who happens to hold them or whether they meet with popular approval. Thirdly. there should be no veto on styles and terms of deliberative engagement, allowing for the equal inclusion of vernacular and affective modes of discourse. Fourthly, deliberators should be constrained by no rules but those to which they have explicitly agreed. Fifthly, there should be no pre-determined outcome to discussion. How might the media help to create these conditions for richly democratic deliberation, as opposed to the vox-populism that usually passes for public political debate?

The media have traditionally seen themselves as *containers* of deliberation. Within their own sacred space of professionally controlled production, the deliberative process is staged for public consumption. As gatekeepers, media professionals see their role as being to guard against quantitative or qualitative disruption: the former when too many voices fight for the power of the microphone; the latter when participants enter the media's sacred space who do not adhere to the standards, protocols, and formats determined by media professionals. Within the logic of the container metaphor, editorial decisions intended to protect deliberation from overload and degeneration make sense. But what if deliberation assumes that all voices should be heard and no elite group is entitled to claim higher knowledge of the public interest? Saward argues that these are indeed definitive requirements of a democracy: that there should be "equal and regular opportunities for all adult citizens to set the public political agenda"[30] because "no single person or minority group can rightfully claim to have an equal or superior insight into the best interests of citizens, either individually or as a whole."[31] Recognizing these principles calls for abandonment of the container metaphor. One can no more organize democratic public communication around the principle of limited, selective rights of entry to media space than one could run democratic elections on the basis that only a few people could ever fit into the polling stations and they could only enter once the electoral officials were convinced that they would make "good voters." There is a fundamental conflict of principle between media gatekeeping and democratic deliberation.

Rather than managing and containing public deliberation, a quite different role for democratic media would be to monitor and make sense of the diverse and distributed political discussions that are taking place within society. Unlike the container model, which places upon the media the formidable responsibility of making deliberation happen, this model of deliberation assumes that public discussion is ubiquitous and incessant. The capacity to reflect upon and talk about social affairs is a defining characteristic of the human animal. Such reflection and talk takes place in diverse ways and is attended by a range of cultural value judgments. Some public talk is dismissed as chat, gossip, storytelling, and banter. Judgments of this kind are rarely ideologically neutral; they have tended to be applied to groups whose interests are deemed to be inferior. So, men put the world to rights, women natter; whites debate history, blacks whine about past injustices; journalists report the news, bloggers circulate rumors. If, however, we are to accept Saward's argument that democracy entails a principled acknowledgment that all voices carry equal weight, a commitment must be made to transcend these ideologically loaded depictions. In Lévinas' terms, democrats cannot allow their prejudices about the Saying to interfere with the deliberative value of what is Said. Indeed, we would go further and argue that not only should public-interest media be open to all voices and values, but they should actively encourage their audiences to adopt a position of openness towards all forms of deliberative input. We are emphatically not arguing here that the media should adopt a kind of relativistic stance which fails to discriminate between statements that are false and valid or rhetoric that is manipulative and innocent. In trying to make sense of the public's deliberations in their varied manifestations – online and offline, formal and informal, political and apolitical – the media should provide responsible interpretations (ideally, many rather than one), but these should follow, rather than preceding or determining, the monitorial function of mapping the ways in which deliberation circulates within and between publics.

If public broadcasters are serious about their aim, as articulated in the BBC's *Building Public Value*, of offering "everyone a democratic voice and a means of contributing to the national debate,"[32] they will need to think beyond current formats revolving around *Question Time*, radio phone-ins and *Have Your Say* message boards. As outlets for free expression and lively entertainment, these formats are not bad – particularly when contrasted with some of the "debate" formats to be found on commercial talk radio. But they are little more than letters' columns of the air and online, allowing a lucky few some precious moments to state the briefest of views before moving on to the next random "voice of the public." Missing from these formats are opportunities for members of the public to debate with one another and for any meaningful linkage between public voice and official decision-making. The parliamentary system of representation emerged at a time when it took hours for messages from most parts of Britain to reach Westminster. In an era of interactive communication, political structures based upon distance and distancing seem increasingly archaic and attempts to appease the distanced public through rhetorics and technologies of spurious inclusion may well exacerbate rather than diminish political efficacy.

Mediating public voice in a politically decentered society has more to do with helping people to find the discussions that relate to them, linking diverse discursive spaces, and providing meta-accounts of public discourses than staging debates and deciding who can join in and who has won the argument. In short, the media's future role in democratic deliberation should be more modest than it has been so far (not arrogating to itself the task of shaping and containing public deliberation), while at the same time it should be more ambitious, seeking deliberative activity in spaces that are not always recognizably political, in the sense that they embrace a certain mode and repertoire conventionally associated with political talk.

Before the political messages emanating from public deliberation can be grasped, made meaningful, and effectively acted upon, the notion of "the political" must be stretched. For, the moment that citizens begin to exchange views, values, and stories about how power affects them and how it should be organized, a space opens up which can be called *the political.* For example, writing about plebiscitary television shows, which find a way to make voting and viewers' choices a part of the show, influencing the outcome of stories or events in the plot, Hartley argues that "it is important not to dismiss voting for pleasure as inconsequential – or worse – without first trying to identify why such activities are popular."[33] Giving the example of young Iranians for whom go-karting is a form of escape from the gender-segregated official public sphere, Hartley argues that ostensibly pleasure-seeking activities can open up spaces for political expression operating next to or across conventional circuits of political discourse. Democratizing public deliberation entails more, therefore, than just a commitment on the part of governing institutions to listen to and learn from those who are able and willing to adopt the language of politics. As sub-culture theorists have long argued, public talk, negotiation, and resistance take many forms which exceed the limits of the official political domain.

But, whether conducted in the recognized lexicon of official politics or through more discrete manifestations, public deliberation cannot be an end in itself. While the experience of deliberating may, as Mill suggested, enable the citizen "to feel for and with his fellow citizens, and become consciously a member of a great community"[34] democratic politics requires that, having established themselves as a self-conscious public, people can make their presence felt in ways that can hold power to account and, indeed, exercise power for themselves.

Speaking Publicly

In a speech on public trust in institutions, Mark Thompson, the Director-General of the BBC, referred to "a charmed circle of knowledge and power" from which the public feels excluded.[35] To be part of the public, in this sense, is to be an outsider, a spectator, permanently dependent upon the perspectives and accounts of others. Public distrust of these perspectives and accounts arises less from disbelief in the accuracy or honesty of media stories than a nagging suspicion that authoritative knowledge is always someone else's and power ever remote.

This image of the public as outsiders, their noses pressed against the thick glass walls which enclose knowledge and power, draws upon a prevalent spatial metaphor. To be a spectator, in this context, is to be morally distanced from the drama of history; to be in a position to observe the appearance of the world, whether directly or via technologies of mediation, but lacking capacity or confidence to intervene in it. The role of spectators as voyeurs, who look on and then look away as their attention wanes, is defined and exhausted by their relationship to the spectacle.

Much has been written about the passivity of spectators. According to Sennett, the spectator was a product of a particular cultural moment in the mid-nineteenth century, when the "public civility established in the *ancien regime*" was superseded by a culture of "passive spectacle."[36] Feeling

> more comfortable as a witness to someone else's expression than as an active conveyor of expression himself, the spectator came to see the world as a performance to be understood, often with the aid of programme notes (for theatre and opera), opinion pieces (for politics) and

etiquette manuals (for everyday interactions.) To be *in public* was to be an outsider entering a complex order of signs, affects, and protocols. Faced with a world not of their own making and cultural powers beyond their influence, spectators "wanted to be told about what they were going to feel [and] what they ought to feel."[37]

Images of the spectator as someone who is "separated from the capacity of knowing just as he is separated from the possibility of acting,"[38] and of the spectacle as a huge and inaccessible reality which cannot be questioned, underpinned early theories of media reception which conceived of audiences as trapped within a system of encoded signals and their inescapable effects. More recent media scholars have rejected this account, attributing active, sense-making roles to spectators and even suggesting a convergence between audiences and publics in the form of "citizen-viewers." The public, in this sense, become active witnesses rather than inert spectators, employing all available techniques and technologies to access, record, circulate, and retell their own accounts of social reality.

Beyond the narrow and diminishing confines of the parochial and interpersonal, the only way that most people can possibly hope to know or be known in the world is through mediated witnessing. In town squares, community halls, local courtrooms, and neighborhood assemblies, everyday provincial dramas are witnessed directly by micro-publics. But the grand and inescapable narratives of national, regional, and global reach are rarely experienced directly. They are mediated in countless ways: via institutional and grass-roots networks, with or without cost, textually and semiotically, monologically and dialogically, plausibly or unconvincingly. The world comes to be known and people's worldliness within it established through witnessing.

The mediated world entails three kinds of witnessing: the object that is witnessed; the subject who witnesses; and the testimony that arises from their encounter.[39] Each of these poses questions of veracity and trust. Does the mediated account truly represent the original event? Can the witnessing subject be trusted to see and understand with any degree of objectivity? Should what is being witnessed be regarded as a self-contained event – or might its unwitnessed history or discretely connected circumstances tell a different story? The work of mediated witnessing, through which we access the appearance and meaning of the world and our position within it, is never reducible to a single objective account.

Witnesses offer plausibility, not absolute truth. The media can only ever offer more or less vivid accounts of social reality, but never an objective or final description.

As we have suggested, the project of nineteenth- and twentieth-century media institutions was to produce and disseminate a final description of social reality, in which the world was witnessed singularly, i.e. by a single public and as a single place. The ironically disposed media of the early twenty-first century seem to be committed to a more inclusive, multi-perspectival approach to witnessing the world. Establishing the terms of public witnessing for a more democratic age of public communication is a pressing challenge for contemporary media – more pressing even than the technical challenges posed by new, digital means of production and dissemination. One aspect of this challenge is highlighted by the contemporary ubiquity of user-generated content within news production. Witness accounts of news events are now commonly dependent upon lay people – non-journalists – who happen to be on the scene of a socially significant event. They take pictures, write blogs, give accounts before TV cameras, and call into radio stations to relate their impressions, rumors, and hunches. Their witnessing of events and our witnessing of their witnessing increasingly constitutes the first draft of history. Yet few standards or protocols are in place to establish how these ongoing, non-institutionalized descriptions of reality can best serve the public interest.

How can forms of mediated witnessing be cultivated that are likely to enhance rather than distract from the principle of a democratic public interest? Defining the public interest as the capacity of the public – and publics – to make their presence felt in ways that can hold power to account, we would argue for four principles of mediated witnessing. As shown below, these principles reflect a sequential process of mediation:

1 call for attention ("I have a story to tell. Is anyone interested?")
2 being understood ("How can I tell you about this in terms that you'll comprehend?")
3 arriving at a public judgment ("Where do we go to form a response to what we've been told that can be spoken in the name of a collective 'us'?")
4 taking consequential action ("What can we do about what we now know?")

Calling for attention

A world in which everyone had their own blog which nobody read, or in which everyone was free to avoid communicating with anyone they did not already know or like, would not be a democracy. It would be an atomized and narcissistic society; an echo chamber rather than a forum. The first principle of democratic communication must be that all people have an opportunity to call for attention from strangers, with some prospect of receiving a response. In its weaker form, this might be equated with the freedom to write a letter to a newspaper, make a call to a phone-in show, or post a message in an online forum. As a stronger right of democratic citizenship, this would entail the opportunity for citizens – and particularly groups – to set agendas for public discussion and would require public institutions to respond to questions and consider proposals emanating from the public. In a mass society, it is never going to be possible for every individual to command the attention of all others, but in democracies there should be ways into the arena of attention-seeking that do not permanently exclude anyone on the grounds of their social status, access to resources, or style of expression. What measures might ensure that this happens?

Firstly, there is a need for an expanded conception of media literacy which takes account of the complexities of entering into the public sphere. This must amount to more than a celebration of technocratic opportunities and officially stated aspirations to overcome "the digital divide." For many people, obstacles to active citizenship have more to do with low self-esteem and lack of political efficacy than access to computers or technical know-how. Inviting people to set up political blogs, post Youtube videos about their communities, or email parliamentary committees with their ideas is of little value if they are left talking to themselves. Levine has rightly expressed concern,

> that we may set kids up for disappointment when we imply that the Internet will make them pamphleteers or broadcasters who can change the world by reaching relevant people. Even if some kids are highly successful, most will *not* draw a significant or appropriate or responsive audience. Most Web sites remain in the tail of the distribution. If you create a site that hardly anyone visits, you will get little feedback. Kids who build such sites may feel that they are failures, especially in a culture that prizes popularity.[40]

In a similar vein (and in the same volume), Rheingold argues that in the blogosphere it is necessary to speak but doing so does not guarantee that you will be heard.[41] He proposes a series of classroom-based exercises designed to teach young people not simply how to use technology, but how to make themselves public by establishing lateral and networked links with others. Citizenship education (or civics), as it has been developed in most countries, shares with programs for media literacy a tendency to prepare its recipients to perform conventional roles (as tax-payers, voters, volunteers, newspaper readers, television viewers) in which civic engagement is enacted through a vertical communication path. Neither citizenship education nor media literacy have paid much attention to forms of horizontal communication. Indeed, they have often sought to steer young people away from them. The need now is to expand media literacy with a view to encouraging network-building practices and skills. Emphasis here would be upon not only being able to access and operate media technologies, but also ways of using them to build publics around issues of common interest; not only sending out signals, but cultivating and responding to the attention of others. Although we refer to this as media literacy, it would involve no less than education for public life. But, unlike nineteenth-century etiquette courses and twentieth-century civics education, the aim here would not be to nurture publics capable of adopting a final vocabulary, but to enable publics to be formed on their own terms.

For this to happen, a second policy must be considered: the need for trusted spaces in which autonomous public-building can take place. As we have said, at a local level these spaces might emerge through regular patterns of social interaction, but on a larger scale public spheres are unlikely to evolve by chance. Democratic public space, in which ideas can be tested, issues of the day debated, and governing institutions held to account, need to be designed as an integral part of the architecture of the contemporary mediascape.

Thirdly, publicly accountable institutions must be compelled to re-think their media strategies, which have tended to be dominated by campaigns to sell their policies to the public in a monological fashion. Some steps have been taken by some parts of some governments to explore the possibilities of interactive dialogue between rulers and ruled, but few of these have led to anything resembling a conversational democracy. As practices and skills of autonomous public-building are more widely acquired and spaces of trusted public communication established, governments will be under enormous pressure to abandon thin and parsimonious conceptions of representation and introduce inventive ways of maintaining an ongoing dialogue about policy values, objectives, priorities, and evaluation. Within the contemporary media profession are thousands of people skilled in making publics laugh, engaging public attention in long-running soap stories, reading and explaining the news, and addressing the tastes of a range of minority audiences. Conspicuously missing from these skills is the ability to translate democracy into a vibrant, inclusive, and multi-vocal experience, characterized by countless calls for attention and an incessant flow of response, discussion, and further linkage. This could prove to be the most significant organizational role for media organizations to perform within a post-centralized democracy.

Making common sense

Public communication is not always about arriving at common understandings. Much communicative energy is devoted to forgetting what is unpleasant or disconcerting, dealing with the embarrassment of misunderstanding, and avoiding the pain of dull, opaque, and futile interaction. Many people go to great lengths to avoid the potential unease of discussions that might result in political disagreement. Politics has come to be equated with manipulation, duplicity, and circumlocution. Indeed, as the BBC Director-General, Mark Thompson, suggests in the speech to which we have already referred, the citizens of modern democracy have come to distrust political discourse, assuming almost as a default position that members of the political elite are "insiders" and that listening to them is a recipe for becoming confused and manipulated:

> Modern public policy is fiendishly complex and debates about it are conducted in a mysterious, technocratic language which – despite the best efforts of the BBC and some of the rest of the media – many people find hard to understand . . . It's not that people . . . feel that all politicians are liars. It's rather that they find much of what politicians say, not just unverifiable, but unintelligible; and that they fear that the system drives politicians and others to distort the truth – and to leave critical parts of it out.[42]

There is much to be said for Thompson's analysis, for it recognizes that visibility alone is no guarantor of political trust. Making voices and images transparent is of little democratic value unless the sense of what is being said and shown is equally transparent. Indeed, people who are most frequently exposed to media coverage of political institutions are least likely to trust them; mediated seeing is not necessarily believing.

For broadcasters, this poses a dilemma: when they offer expert analysis of complex political issues they are accused of elitist indifference towards the majority of their audience; when they seek to introduce complex stories in popular and accessible ways they are accused of "dumbing down." Both of these accusations are too simplistic. Firstly, because, as in all aspects of mediation, there is room for more than one explanatory style. For example, the four-yearly coverage of the Olympic Games addresses both sports' devotees who will have watched and participated in particular games throughout the non-Olympic years, and people with a passing interest in great sporting occasions whose attention is only likely to be held if the rules and dramas of the game are explained before they can be fully engaged. Such explanation is not "dumbing down," but can be interpreted as a form of hospitality – in much the same way as a restaurant selling French wines might provide hospitable translations for the benefit of non-French speakers or non-wine-drinkers, or a professor giving a lecture might begin by defining the more difficult or contested terms that she proposes to use. There is a certain kind of authority that depends upon the unease of those subjected to it. Democratic authority is not of this kind.

A second reason for casting doubt upon the elitist–dumbed-down dichotomy is that the public comprises neither homogeneously informed nor uninformed elements. Many of those who regard themselves as politically well informed possess a relatively narrow range of knowledge, often related to political parties, economic affairs, and a small number of countries. Many people who do not read a daily newspaper or follow conventional politics have a lot to say about power as exercised in their own communities or workplaces or families. Some of them will be prepared to speak actively about the political implications of supporting a musical genre or objecting to offensive behavior on television or subscribing to particular online networks, even though they will not think of these contexts as having anything to do with "politics." Different groups articulate their knowledge in contrasting ways and, because traditional political participators tend to share a language and grammar with journalists and politicians, they tend to be taken more seriously. Advocates of final vocabularies tend to be intolerant of pluralistic accounts and readings of notions such as news, citizenship, politics, or significance. A democratic media environment should disdain instant dismissals of the value of particular interests, discourses, narratives, or explanations.

This leads to a third and final reason to think more imaginatively about ways of producing common sense. The prevailing geographical metaphor, which places people as insiders and outsiders, is based upon an implicit model of contained and centralized power. In the media context, this image has been supplemented by dramaturgical metaphors of "stage" and "audience." These metaphors have tended to frame rather than describe contemporary social relationships; that is to say, they have become implicit models for the organization of political and symbolic power. In a post-industrial and post-deferential society, competing models of public communication need to be taken seriously. Whereas the nineteenth-century spectators described by Sennett went to the theater in fear of misunderstanding the high-cultural signals they were there to ingest, and lower-middle-class newspaper readers would arm themselves with dictionaries in order to keep up with the high-table discourse of celebrated columnists, the public interest in a democratic era is more likely to be served by forms of witnessing in which efforts to comprehend are shared equally. Politicians now devote considerable energy to be seen not only to address public interests, but to do so in terms that show a respect and affinity for popular culture. Media producers who once saw it as their business to define (and often defy) popular taste are increasingly eager to position themselves as professional witnesses at the theater of everyday life, simulating it in soaps, replicating it in reality TV formats, and reporting on public experience as part of daily news. Public life has become the new "inside" acted upon in various ways by political and media technologies that operate within "a global field" comprising a "system of local fields, their distributions and linkages."[43]

The post-authoritarian media ecology is characterized by dialectical interaction between the local and the universal, presence and distance, agency and structure, and a range of tensions between immediate experience and mediated understanding. In this context, there remains abundant room for miscommunication, asymmetrical knowledge, and the embarrassment of not knowing or being known, but there is also scope for a more open acknowledgment of and reflection upon these barriers to common understanding. Providing a space for the articulation and negotiation of disputed meanings is a key role to be performed by democratic media. Rather than the unedifying ways in which populist tabloids and some broadcasters have sought to crowd out images and perspectives that disrupt their view of the world, and even the professedly enlightened media belittle the voices of the least confident or articulate, the pressing need for contemporary democracies is to facilitate diverse and mutually respecting forms of sense-making. The communicative spaces opened up by digital media (discussed in Chapter 5) have to some extent unsettled the prescriptive hegemony of the mass media by affording important opportunities for hidden scripts to be revealed, shared, and celebrated. But can these be transformed into collective judgments?

Generating public opinion(s)

How, then, can people not only make sense of the mediated world they witness, but arrive at judgments that can be spoken in the name of the public? Attempts to discover public opinion have most commonly been based upon the snapshot method of opinion polling. As a social technology, the objective of polling is to produce an aggregated public comprised of a sample of individual views deemed to be scientifically representative of a particular population. Polling-generated publics do not come into being through their own volition, but in response to the demand of others to know about them. Atomized individuals are selected for questioning. Neither the theme nor the form of the questions asked are determined by the poll respondents, whose task is to react to themes that others have determined to make public.

Pollsters are generally uninterested in how respondents have arrived at their judgments or whether the views that they describe as public opinion are based upon knowledge or misconception, altruism or selfishness, discussion with others or isolated brooding, or, indeed, any real comprehension of what the pollsters meant by their questions. Opinion polls are, like the script for a theatrical chorus, uniform and crude. As in a chorus, when one actor is given a momentary speaking part, their role is always to articulate typicality: if the chorus is scared, she utters sounds of pathetic fear; if the chorus is joyful, the only permissible purpose of her words can be to express this collective mood.

So, when well executed, opinion polls generate reactive publics whose role is to act in accordance with an aggregately produced script. Sadly for pollsters and those who place too much faith in their findings, real-world publics behave anomalously, defying the neatness of the surveyors' science. People often hold more than one opinion about the same issue, but these inconsistencies are rarely captured by pollsters. Indeed, some opinions are regarded as embarrassing, stigmatizing, or simply too personal, and poll respondents therefore pretend not to hold them. For these and other reasons, all that one can say of most opinion polls is that they provide a snapshot of how a particular group of people respond to the situation of being faced with a set of questions that are not of their own making.

The most worrying aspect of polling, as a guide to public judgment, is its ahistorical perspective. By definition, a snapshot is instantaneous; like a photograph of a happy family, it cannot illuminate the miseries, abuses, misunderstandings, inequalities, and pretences that led up to the contrived moment of representation. Longitudinal polling, which is expensive and rare, sometimes captures a more nuanced sense of fluctuating conditions, but it can never explain them or allow those experiencing them to speak of them. The snapshot-recorded public, like the theater chorus, is historically dumb; it has a past, but no means of engaging with it.

At its best, therefore, polling is a way of ascribing thoughts to the public. To be polled or surveyed is to be invited to respond so that one can be spoken about. It is not an autonomous act of self-expression, but an observational technique employed in order to describe those who exist outside the portals of official knowledge and power. In contrast to this endless scrutiny of the public as "them" are forms of articulation that enable people to speak of "us." One key function of democratic media is to facilitate such articulations by being sensitive and open to the countless ways in which people use the word "us" to describe their experiences, aspirations, fears, beliefs, and projections. A second equally vital function is to create links between diverse and distinct publics so that, if not all or even most of the time, there can be occasions on which they can interact as a mutually communicating public. Some public judgments are most likely to emerge out of shared histories and values, while others, of a more universal nature, can only be arrived at through the sometimes uncomfortable meeting of conflicting histories and values. The moral task of democratic media is to facilitate such public meetings, across distances of space, history, and affect, in ways that allow the word "us" to be used as broadly and unthreateningly as possible. The BBC's declared aim of "enabling the UK's many communities to see what they hold in common and how they differ" is an important move in the right direction. But, beyond *seeing* one another, the media must enable people to act upon what they witness by moving towards judgments about the public interest.

This brings us back to the contrasting roles of spectators and witnesses. The former are united by a common gaze, but atomized at the point of reflection and judgment. As Debord famously put it, spectators are "linked only by a one-way relationship to the very centre that maintains their isolation from one another."[44] Witnesses, on the other hand, only come into their own when they are in a position to appeal to the judgment of others. Just as a witness to a crime who remained indifferent to whether others believed his account and refused to testify in court would be doomed to irrelevance, so mediated witnessing is only of any value in the context of socialized judgment-making. For, as Peters points out, "to witness an event is to be responsible in some way to it."[45] This holds true not only for our assessment of the veracity of mediated witness accounts, but for the judgments that we make about them. In liberal democracies, based upon the inviolable principle that "no single person or minority group can rightfully claim to have an equal or superior insight into the best interests of citizens, either individually or as a whole,"[46] no witness, claimant, or advocate should be regarded as possessing innately privileged access to what constitutes the public interest. Throughout most of their history, media organizations, including public service broadcasters like the BBC, have dismissed that democratic principle, in deed if not in words. Contributing to a post-authoritarian culture in which the public interest no longer describes an elitist conception of what's good for people, but the self-articulated needs and desires of the people themselves, is not simply a policy option for the media in contemporary democracies. It is a prerequisite for any democratic conception of the public interest.

Making a difference

We are asking a great deal of the media. Help us to encounter one another as real people. Enable is to meet other publics and enter other spaces that have been too easily and casually made invisible in the past. Acknowledge and reflect the countless deliberations, conversations, whispers, and silences that constitute an already existing public dialogue about who we are and what we want. And ensure that publics are able to speak for themselves, calling to the attention of others, making themselves understood, and arriving at common judgments about their own interests. Some people would say that that is precisely what the media do right now. We hope that we have shown in previous chapters that these democratic norms are beset by problems.

The most conspicuous of these problems is illuminated by a glaring paradox of contemporary democracies: people appear to have more opportunities than ever before to question their rulers, challenge official information, contribute to mainstream media, produce their own media, speak for themselves, and act as they wish in public – and yet everywhere people report feeling distant from elites, ignored by the media, unheard by representatives, constrained in public speech, and utterly frustrated by the promises of democracy. People do not want to get rid of democracy. They want it to be taken seriously. *They* want to be taken seriously. But they despair about their ability to make a difference.

At the most basic level, this lack of efficacy feels very much like being cheated. For example, in recent years millions of people have been persuaded to pay their own money to participate in phone votes with a view to determining the outcomes of programs. And then it was discovered that many of these were rigged so that the only votes that really counted were those consistent with the intentions of producers. Commenting on an inquiry into this corruption, Michael Grade, the then head of ITV, acknowledged that "It was not understood that when the audience is invited to make choices within programs, the producer is effectively ceding part of his/her sovereignty over editorial decisions."[47] In short, even the most elementary move in the direction of media democracy affects the distribution of power.

Media organizations are embedded in structures of power, but do not constitute them. The capacity of the public to make a difference through their actions does not depend only upon institutional compliance by the media. The extent to which societies open up, use, and respect public space is determined by their confidence in looking one another in the eye. The media are both a reflection of that confidence, or lack of it, and a generator of it. They can shut down what is public by disparaging everyday speech and behavior, spreading fear of human interaction, fetishizing the political spectacle, and drawing bleak conclusions about the capacity for social solidarity. Or they can see publicness as a setting for creative ingenuity, chatty sociability, honest deliberation, and the celebration of differences. The aim of this book has been to clarify these choices, while arguing throughout that democracy must mean the capacity of the public to make a difference for itself.

Notes

Introduction

1 Claude Lefort (1986) *The Political Forms of Modern Society*. Cambridge, MA: MIT Press: 279.
2 John B. Thompson (1995) *The Media and Modernity: A Social Theory of the Media*. Cambridge: Polity Press: 126.

1 Imagining the Public

1 Michael Warner (2002) *Publics and Counterpublics*. Cambridge, MA: MIT Press: 65.
2 John Hartley (2007) *Television Truths: Forms of Knowledge in Popular Culture*. Malden, MA: Blackwell: 1.
3 Clive Barnett (2003) *Culture and Democracy: Media, Space and Representation*. Edinburgh: Edinburgh University Press: 4.
4 Paddy Scannell (2004) *Big Brother* as a television event. *New Media and Society* 3(3): 271–282.
5 John S. McClelland (1998) *A History of Western Political Thought*. London and New York: Routledge: 3–4.
6 Hippolyte Taine (1881/1972) *The Ancient Regime* (trans. John Durand). Freeport, NY: Books for Libraries Press: 241.
7 Thomas Carlyle (1897) *Latter-day Pamphlets. Chartism*. Boston: deWolfe, Fiske: 6.
8 John Halperin (1982) *Gissing: A Life in Books*. Oxford: Oxford University Press: 100 and 295.
9 Gustave Le Bon (1895, 1991) *Psychologie des foules*. Paris: PUF.: xx, trans. Robert Nye.

10 Cited in Henry Jephson (1892) *The Platform: Its Rise and Progress*, vol. 1. London: Macmillan: 190.

11 Cited in John Plotz (2000) *The Crowd: British Literature and Public Politics*. Berkeley, CA: University of California Press.

12 Ibid.

13 Daniel Dayan (2005) Mothers, midwives and abortionists: genealogy, obstetrics, audiences and publics. In Sonia Livingstone (ed.) *Audiences and Publics: When Cultural Engagement Matters for the Public Sphere*. Bristol: Intellect.

14 Walter Bagehot (1872) *The English Constitution*. Online at http://bagehot. classicauthors.net/EnglishConstitution/EnglishConstitution1.html (accessed 29 September 2009).

15 Nikolas Rose (1999) *The Powers of Freedom*. Cambridge: Cambridge University Press: 200.

16 Susan Herbst (1993) *Numbered Voices: How Opinion Polling Has Shaped American Politics*. Chicago: University of Chicago Press: 133–151.

17 Herbert Blumer (1948) Public opinion and public opinion polling. *American Sociological Review* 13(5): 542–549; P. Bourdieu (1971) Public opinion does not exist. In A. Matelart and S. Siegelaub (eds.) *Communication and Class Struggle* (New York: International General/IMMRC): 224.

18 Sidney Verba (1996) The citizen as respondent: sample surveys and American democracy. Presidential address, American Political Science Association, 1995. *American Political Science Review* 90(1): 1.

19 Benjamin Ginsberg (1998) *The Captive Public: How Mass Opinion Promotes State Power*. New York: Basic Books: 293.

20 Charles Tilly (1983) Speaking your mind without elections, surveys or social movements. *Public Opinion Quarterly* 47(4): 474.

21 Rose, *The Powers of Freedom*: 208.

22 Michael Pickering and David Chaney (1986) Democracy and communication: Mass Observation. *Journal of Communication* 36(1): 42.

23 Penny Summerfield (1985) Mass Observation: social research or social movement? *Journal of Contemporary History* 20(3): 448.

24 Barnett, *Culture and Democracy*: 5.

25 Warner, *Publics and Counterpublics*: 76.

26 Ibid.: 88.

27 Ibid.: 114.

28 Ibid.: 113.

29 Ien Ang (1995) *Living Room Wars: Rethinking Media Audiences for a Postmodern World*. London: Routledge: 35.

30 Livingstone, *Audiences and Publics*: 211.

31 Zygmunt Bauman (2000) *Liquid Modernity*. Cambridge: Polity Press: 71.

32   John Ellis (2000) *Seeing Things: Television in the Age of Uncertainty*. London: I.B. Tauris: 9.

33   John Durham Peters (2001) Witnessing. *Media, Culture and Society* 23(6): 709.

34   Anthony Giddens (1991) *Modernity and Self-Identity*. Cambridge: Polity Press: 187.

35   Margaret Kohn (2003) *Radical Space*. Ithaca, NY: Cornell University Press: 3–4.

36   M. Foucault (2002) *Archaeology of Knowledge*. New York and London: Routledge.

37   Don Mitchell (1995) The end of public space? People's Park, definitions of the public and democracy. *Annals of the Association of American Geographers* 85(1): 108–133.

38   *Hansard*, May 27, 1866, vol. 175: 769–777.

39   *The Times*, July 24, 1866.

40   *Hansard*, 13 August, 1867.

41   Ibid.

42   Hannah Arendt (1958) *The Human Condition*. Chicago: Chicago University Press: 194.

43   Benedict Anderson (1991) *Imagined Communities: Reflections on the Origin and Spread of Nationalism*. London: Verso.

44   I. Kant (1781/2007) *Critique of Pure Reason*. London: Penguin.

45   Jürgen Habermas (1996) *Between Facts and Norms: Contributions to a Discourse Theory of Law and Democracy*. Cambridge, MA: MIT Press: 360.

46   Oskar Negt and Alexander Kluge (1993) *Public Sphere and Experience: Toward an Analysis of the Bourgeois and Proletarian Public Sphere*. Minneapolos, MN: University of Minnesota Press: 2.

47   Thompson, *Media and Modernity*: 123.

48   *Order and Usage howe to keepe a Parliament*, 1571.

49   Thompson, *Media and Modernity*: 245, emphasis in original.

2   Public Spheres

1   Jürgen Habermas (1991) *The Structural Transformation of the Public Sphere: An Inquiry Into a Category of Bourgeois Society*. Cambridge, MA: MIT Press: 53.

2   Anthony J. La Vopa (1992) Conceiving a public: ideas and society in eighteenth-century Europe. *Journal of Modern History* 64(10): 80.

3   Mona Ozouf (1989) *L'homme régénéré: Essais sur la révolution française*. Paris: Gallimard: S11.

4 Cited in Lucy Kung-Shackleman (2000) *Inside the BBC and CNN*. London and New York: Routledge: 70.

5 Ibid.

6 Paddy Scannell and David Cardiff (1991) *A Social History of British Broadcasting*, vol. 1: *1922–39: Serving the Nation*, Oxford: Blackwell: 158.

7 Cited in Michael Gurevitch (1982) *Culture, Society, and the Media*. London and New York: Routledge: 302.

8 Asa Briggs (1985) *The BBC: A Short Story of the First Fifty Years*. Oxford: Oxford University Press: 151.

9 Paddy Scannell (2000) For-anyone-as-someone structures. *Media, Culture and Society*, 23(1): 5–24.

10 Ibid.: 9.

11 www.bookrags.com/research/true-story-magazine-sjpc-04/ (accessed 29 September 2009).

12 Erving Goffman (1981) *Forms of Talk*. Oxford: Blackwell.

13 Donald Horton and Richard R. Wohl (1956) Mass communication and para-social interaction: observations on intimacy at a distance. *Psychiatry* 19(3): 215.

14 Scannell and Cardiff, *A Social History of British Broadcasting*, vol. 1: 174.

15 Wilfred Pickles (1950) *Between You and Me*. London: Werner Laurie: 84.

16 Laurie Ouellette (2002) *Viewers Like You? How Public TV Failed the People*. New York: Columbia University Press: 121.

17 John Dewey (1927) *The Public and its Problems*. London: H. Holt & Co.

18 Bertolt Brecht (1936) Radiotheorie 1927–1932. *Gesammelte Werke Band*, 1: 117–124. The translated text appears in Hans Magnus Enzensberger (1970) Constituents of a theory of the media. www.religion-online.org/showarticle.asp?title=1567 (accessed 29 September 2009).

19 Hans Magnus Enzensberger (1970) Constituents of a theory of the media. *New Left Review* 1: 64.

20 Raymond Williams (1961) *Culture and Society, 1780–1950*. London: Penguin Books: 117–121.

21 Brian Groombridge (1972) *Television and the People*. London: Penguin: 14.

22 Ibid.

23 UNESCO (1980) *Many Voices One World: Towards a New, More Just and More Efficient World Information and Communication Order* (the "MacBride Commission."), Lanham, MD: Rowman & Littlefield: 171.

24 ibid.: 173, 174.

25 John Downing (2001) *Radical Media: Rebellious Communication and Social Movements*. London and New York: Sage: 16.

26 Ibid.: 31.

27 Bernard Manin (1997) *The Principles of Representative Government*. Cambridge: Cambridge University Press.

28   www.publicaccesstv.net/history02.html.
29   Amitai Etzioni (1972) MINERVA: An electronic town hall. *Policy Sciences* 3(4): 18.

3   The Managed Public

1   John B. Thompson (1995) *The Media and Modernity: A Social Theory of the Media*. Cambridge: Polity Press: 32.
2   A. Giddens (1990) *The Consequences of Modernity*, Cambridge: Polity Press.
3   Ien Ang (1991) *Desperately Seeking the Audience*. London: Routledge, 17–18.
4   Andrew Graham (2000) *The Future of Communications: Public Service Broadcasting*. Luton: University of Luton Press.
5   Cory L. Armstrong (2004) The influence of reporter gender on source selection in newspaper stories. *Journalism and Mass Communication Quarterly* 81(1): 139–154.
6   Karen Ross. (2007) The journalist, the housewife, the citizen and the press: women and men as sources in local news narratives. *Journalism* 8(4): 449–514.
7   John E. Richardson (2001) "Now is the time to put an end to all this": argumentative discourse theory and "letters to the editor." *Discourse and Society* 12(2): 143–168.
8   Ross, The journalist, the housewife, the citizen and the press.
9   Erik Bucy and Kimberly Gregson (2001) Media participation: a legitimizing mechanism of mass democracy. *New Media and Society* 3(2): 375–376.
10   Karin Wahl-Jorgensen (2002) The construction of the public in letters to the editor: deliberative democracy and the idiom of insanity. *Journalism* 3(2): 183–204.
11   Ibid.
12   Graham Murdock (1999) Rights and representations; public discourse and cultural citizenship. In Jostein Gripsrud (ed.) *Television and Common Knowledge*. London: Routledge: 14.
13   Bucy and Gregson, Media participation: 375–376.
14   Sonia Livingstone and Peter Lunt (1994) *Talk on Television*. London: Routledge: 36.
15   Paulo Carpignano et al. (1990) Chatter in the age of electronic reproduction: talk television and the public mind. In Bruce Robbins (ed.) *The Phantom Public Sphere*. Minneapolis: University of Minnesota Press: 93–120.
16   Murdock, Rights and representations: 14.

17 Paddy Scannell (1996) *Radio, Television, and Modern Life: A Phenomeno-logical Approach*. Oxford: Blackwell: 76.
18 Carpignano et al. (1990) Chatter in the age of electronic reproduction.
19 Helen Wood (2007) The mediated conversational floor: an interactive approach to audience reception analysis. *Media, Culture and Society* 29(1): 75–103 at p. 79.
20 Ibid.

4 Counterpublics and Alternative Media

1 Oskar Negt and Alexander Kluge (1993) *Public Sphere and Experience: Toward an Analysis of the Bourgeois and Proletarian Public Sphere*. Minneapolis: University of Minnesota Press.
2 Rita Felski (1989) *Beyond Feminist Aesthetic: Feminist Literature and Social Change*. London: Radius.
3 Robert Asen (2000) Seeking the "counter" in counterpublics. *Communication Theory* 10(4): 425.
4 Brett Hutchins and Libby Lester (2006) Environmental protest and tap-dancing with the media in the information age. *Media, Culture and Society* 28(3): 433–451.
5 Glasgow University Media Group (1976) *Bad News*. London: Routledge & Kegan Paul; (1982) *Really Bad News*. London: Routledge & Kegan Paul; (1985) *War and Peace News*. Milton Keynes: Open University Press.
6 www.tlio.org.uk/pubs/index.html (accessed September 24, 2006).
7 Polyanna Ruiz (2005) Bridging the gap: from the margins to the mainstream. In Wilma de Jong, Martin Shaw, and Neil Stammers (eds.) *Global Activism, Global Media*. London, Ann Arbor, MI: Pluto Press: 194–207.
8 Sara Berger (2005) From Aldermaston marcher to Internet activist. In Wilma de Jong, Martin Shaw, and Neil Stammers (eds.) *Global Activism, Global Media*. London, Ann Arbor, MI: Pluto Press: 91.
9 Ivor Gaber and A. Wynne Willson (2005) Dying for diamonds: the mainstream media and NGOs – A case study of Action Aid. In Wilma de Jong, Martin Shaw, and Neil Stammers (eds.) *Global Activism, Global Media*. London, Ann Arbor, MI: Pluto Press: 95–109.
10 Royal Commission on the Press (1977). London: HMSO: 40.
11 Mitzi Waltz (2005) *Alternative and Activist Media*. Edinburgh: Edinburgh University Press.
12 Chris Atton (2002) *Alternative Media*. London: Sage: 27.
13 Kevin Howley (2003) A poverty of voices: street newspapers as communicative democracy. *Journalism* 4(3): 273–292.

14 Tessa Swithinbank (1996) World exclusive. *New Internationalist*. February: 28–30.

15 "Jane," cited in Patricia L. Gibbs (2003) Alternative things considered: a political economic analysis of labour processes and relations at a Honolulu alternative newspaper. *Media, Culture and Society* 25(5): 579.

16 Stephen Duncombe (1996) *Notes from Underground: Zines and the Politics of Alternative Culture*. London: Verso.

17 Kristen Schilt (2003) "I'll resist with every inch and every breath." Girls and zine-making as a form of resistance. *Youth and Society* 35(1): 71–97.

18 Nicholas Jankowski (2002) The conceptual contours of community radio. In Nicholas Jankowski with Ole Prehn (2002) *Community Media in the Information Age: Perspectives and Prospects*. Cresskill, NJ: Hampton Press: 7–8.

19 Bruce Girard (ed.) (1992) *A Passion for Radio: Radio Waves and Community*. Montreal: Black Rose Books: ix.

20 Donald R. Browne (2005) *Ethnic Minorities, Electronic Media and the Public Sphere: A Comparative Approach*. Cresskill, NJ: Hampton Press.

21 Waltz (2005) *Alternative and Activist Media*.

22 www.kpfa.org (accessed September 29, 2009).

23 Waltz, *Alternative and Activist Media*.

24 Dunifer quoted in ibid.: 63.

25 Susan Forde, Kerrie Foxwell, and Michael Meadows (2003) Through the lens of the local: public arena: journalism in the Australian community broadcasting sector. *Journalism* 4(3): 314–335.

26 Birgitte Jallov (1992) Community radio as a tool for feminist messages. In Nicholas Jankowski, Ole Prehn, and J. Stappers (eds.) *The People's Voice: Local Radio and Television in Europe*. Luton: John Libbey & Co: 216.

27 Scéal = gossip, stories.

28 Caroline Mitchell (2000) Sisters are doing it . . . from Fem FM to Viva! A history of contemporary women's radio stations in the UK. In Caroline Mitchell (ed.) *Women and Radio: Airing Differences*. London and New York: Routledge.

29 Ibid.: 95–96.

30 Sally Feldman (2000) Twin peaks: the staying power of BBC Radio 4's *Woman's Hour*. In Caroline Mitchell (ed.) *Women and Radio: Airing Differences*. London and New York: Routledge: 64.

31 Browne, *Ethnic Minorities, Electronic Media and the Public Sphere*.

32 George L. Daniels (2006) The role of Native American print and online media in the "era of big stories": a comparative case study of Native American outlets' coverage of the Red Lake shootings. *Journalism* 7(3): 321–342.

33 Susan Forde (1998) The development of the alternative press in Australia. *Media International Australia* 87:114–133.

34 Tokunbo Ojo (2006) Ethnic print media in the multicultural nation of Canada: a case study of the black newspaper in Montreal. *Journalism* 7(3): 343–361.

5 Virtual Publicness

1 *Time*, December 13, 2006.
2 Dan Gillmor (2004) *We the Media: Grassroots Journalism by the People, for the People*. Sebastopol, CA: O'Reilly.
3 Shane Bowman and Chris Willis (2003) *We Media: How Audiences are Shaping the Future of News and Information*. Reston, VA: The Media Center at the American Press Institute.
4 John Perry Barlow (1996) A Declaration of the Independence of Cyberspace. Online at http://homes.eff.org/~barlow/Declaration-Final.html (accessed August 20, 2008).
5 Bruce Allen Bimber (1996) *Politics of Expertise in Congress: Rise and Fall of the Office of Technology Assessment*. New York: State University of New York Press: 92; emphasis in the original.
6 The Bodleian Library, which includes copies of all books published since the early seventeenth century, contains approximately eight million items on 117 miles of shelving. As of July 2008, Google had indexed one trillion web pages.
7 Axel Bruns (2005) *Gatewatching: Collaborative Online News Production*. Oxford: Peter Lang: 2.
8 www.mcspotlight.org (accessed October 1, 2006).
9 www.mcspotlight.org/people/interviews/morris97.html (accessed October 1, 2006).
10 www.mcspotlight.org/media/press/msc_31mar99.html (accessed October 1, 2006).
11 Yochai Benkler (2006) *The Wealth of Networks: How Social Production Transforms Markets and Freedom*. New Haven, CT: Yale University Press: 291.
12 Clay Shirky (2005) Ontology is overrated: categories, links and tags. Online at www.shirky.com/writings/ontology_overrated.htm (accessed August 20, 2008).
13 John Fiske (1987) *Television Culture*. London and New York: Routledge.
14 Matthew Arnison (2001) Open publishing is the same as free software. Online at www.cat.org.au/maffew/cat/openpub.html (accessed May 8, 2009).
15 John B. Thompson (2005) The new visibility. *Theory, Culture and Society* 22(1): 31.

16 Andy Carvin, How the Internet is changing the playing field. Online at www. america.gov/st/usg-english/2008/April/20080523104429WRybakcuHO. 324383.html (accessed September 21, 2009).

17 Jean Burgess (2006) Hearing ordinary voices. *Continuum* 20(2): 201–214 at p. 204.

18 http://urbantapestries.net/

19 Michael Pickering and David Chaney (1986) Democracy and communication: Mass Observation. *Journal of Communication* 36(1): 42.

20 Robert Kraut et al. (1998) Coordination and virtualization: the role of electronic networks and personal relationships. *Journal of Computer-Mediated Communication* 3(4). Online at www3.interscience.wiley.com/cgi-bin/fulltext/120837744/HTMLSTART (accessed September 15, 2008).

21 Norman Nie, and Lutz Erbring (2000, March). Internet and society: a preliminary report. Online at www.stanford.edu/group/siqss/Press_Release/Preliminary_Report.pdf (accessed July 28, 2008).

22 David Altheide (1995) *An Ecology of Communication: Cultural Formats of Control*, New York: Aldine: 101.

23 Anabel Quan-Haase and Barry Wellman (2004) How does the Internet affect social capital? In Marleen Hysman and Volker Wulf (eds.) *Social Capital and Information Technology*. Cambridge, MA. MIT Press: 113–132.

24 Barry Wellman, Jeffrey Boase, and Wenhans Chen (2002) The networked nature of community online and offline. *IT and Society* 1(1): 1–15.

25 Andrea L. Kavanaugh and Scott J. Patterson (2001) The impact of community computer networks on social capital and community involvement. *American Behavioral Scientist* (45)3: 496–509; Bernhard Krieger and Phillip S. Muller (2003) Making internet communities work: reflections on an unusual business model. *ACM SIGMIS Database* 34(2): 50–59.

26 Dhavan V. Shah, Nojin Kwak, and R. Lance Holbert (2001) "Connecting" and "disconnecting" with civic life: patterns of Internet use and the production of social Capital. *Political Communication* 18(2): 154.

27 Ibid.

28 Thomas J. Johnson and Barbara Kaye (2003) Around the World Wide Web in 80 ways: how motives for going online are linked to Internet activities among politically interested Internet users. *Social Science Computer Review* 21(3): 304–325 at p. 310.

29 W. Lance Bennett, (2003) New media power: the Internet and global activism. In Nick Couldry and James Curran (eds.) *Contesting Media Power: Alternative Media in a Networked World*. Lanham, MD: Rowman & Littlefield: 14.

30 Personal interview with Stephen Coleman, 200?. http://www.kikass.tv/ (accessed 31 March 2009).

31 Representative of Leeds University Students Union in personal interview with Stephen Coleman, 200?.

32 Andrew Chadwick (2006) *Internet Politics: States, Citizens and New Communication Technologies.* New York and Oxford: Oxford University Press.

33 Bertolt Brecht (1932) Der Rundfunk als Kommunikationsapparat. *Bjitter des Hessischen Landestheaters Darmstadt* 16, July.

34 Neil Postman (1985) *Amusing Ourselves to Death,* New York: Viking.

35 Stephen Coleman and Giles Moss (2008) Governing at a distance: politicians in the blogosphere. *Information Polity* 13(1–2): 7–20.

36 Irina Shklovski, Robert Kraut, and Lee Rainie (2004) The Internet and social participation: contrasting cross-sectional and longitudinal analyses. *Journal of Computer Mediated Communication* 10(1). Online at http://jcmc.indiana.edu/vol10/issue1/shklovski_kraut.html (accessed September 9, 2008).

37 Jeffrey Boase and Barry Wellman (2006) Personal relationships: on and off the Internet. In Anita L. Vengelisti and Daniel Perlman (eds.) *The Cambridge Handbook of Personal Relationships.* Cambridge: Cambridge University Press: 709–726.

38 Mary Power, Des Power, and Louise Horstmanshof (2007) Deaf people communicating via SMS, TTY, relay service, fax, and computers in Australia. *Journal of Deaf Studies and Deaf Education,* 12(1): 82.

39 Peter Millward (2008) The rebirth of the football fanzine: using e-zines as data source. *Journal of Sport and Social Issues* 32(3): 299–310.

40 S. Coleman and Jay G. Blumler (2008) *The Internet and Democratic Citizenship: Theory, Practice and Policy.* Cambridge: Cambridge University Press: see especially chapter 5.

41 Simon Buckingham-Shum, (2007) Hypermedia discourse: contesting networks of ideas and arguments. In Uta Priss, Simon Polovina, and Richard Hill (eds.) *Conceptual Structures: Knowlede Architectures for Smart Applications. Proceedings of the 15th International Conference on Conceptual Structures.* Berlin: Springer-Verlag: 29–44. Online at www.springerlink.com/content/x16xr44xp680/?p=165e5f2693254571992406f8a01af936&pi=0 (accessed September 10, 2008).

42 www.medienkunstnetz.de/works/conversation-map/ (accessed May 8, 2009). See also Warren Sack (2000) Conversation Map: an interface for very large-scale conversations. *Journal of Management Information Systems* 17(3): 73–92.

43 Michael B. MacKuen (1990) Speaking of politics: individual conversational choice, public opinion, and the prospects for deliberative democracy. In John A. Ferejohn and James H. Kuklinski (eds.) *Information and Democratic Processes.* Urbana, IL: University of Illinois Press: 101.

44 Jay G. Blumler and Stephen Coleman (2001) *Realising Democracy Online: A Civic Commons in Cyberspace.* London: Institute of Public Policy Research: 5–6.

45 Stephen Coleman (2004) Connecting Parliament to the public via the Internet. *Information, Communication and Society* 7(1): 1–22.
46 Jamal Shahin and Christine Neuhold (2007) Connecting Europe: the use of "new" information and communication technologies within European Parliament Standing Committees. *Journal of Legislative* Studies 13(3): 388–402.
47 *Adapted from Democracies Online Case Study List: http://dowire.org/wiki/ Listening_to_the_City.*
48 www.internetworldstats.com/stats.htm. (accessed May 7, 2009).
49 Yochai Benkler (2006) *The Wealth of Networks: How Social Production Transforms Markets and Freedom.* New Haven, CT: Yale University Press: 000.
50 Manuel Castells (2000) *The Rise of the Network Society: The Information Age: Economy, Society and Culture* vol. 1. Malden, MA: Wiley-Blackwell.
51 Benkler (2006) *The Wealth of Networks.*
52 Peter Dahlgren (2005) The Internet, public spheres, and political communication: dispersion and deliberation. *Political Communication,* 22(2): 150.
53 Cass Sunstein (2001) Democracy and the Internet. *Mots Pluriel* 18, August. Online at www.arts.uwa.edu.au/MotsPluriels/MP1801cs.html (accessed August 20, 2008).
54 Craig Calhoun (2007) Community without propinquity revisited: communications technology and the transformation of the urban public sphere. *Sociological Inquiry,* 68(3): 375.
55 Sunstein, Democracy and the Internet.
56 Daniel W. Drezner and Henry Farrell (2008) Introduction: Blogs, politics and power. *Public Choice* 134: 1–13.
57 Ibid.
58 Wanda Orlikowski (1992) Learning from Notes: organizational issues in groupware implementation. Computer-supported cooperative work. *Proceedings of the 1992 ACM Conference on Computer-Supported Work.* Ontario: Association of Computer Machinery: 36.
59 Richard Sennett (1992) *The Fall of Public Man.* New York: W.W. Norton: xi.

6 Fractured Publics, Contested Publicness

1 David Morrison et al. (2007) *Media and Values: Intimate Transgressions in a Changing Moral and Cultural Landscape.* London: Intellect: 263.
2 Richard Rorty (1989) *Contingency, Irony, and Solidarity.* Cambridge: Cambridge University Press: 74.
3 Ibid.: 73.
4 Roger Silverstone (2007) *Media and Morality: On the Rise of the Mediapolis.* Cambridge: Polity Press: 28.

5   John C.W. Reith (1949) *Into the Wind: Memoirs.* London: Hodder & Stoughton: 136.

6   Ibid.: 5.

7   Asa Briggs (1961) *The Birth of Broadcasting.* Oxford: Oxford University Press: 265.

8   BBC (2004) *Building Public Value: Renewing the BBC for a Digital World.* London: BBC: 6.

9   Ibid.: 14.

10 Raymond Williams (1961) *Culture and Society, 1780–1950.* London: Penguin Books: 304.

11 Ibid.: 301.

12 Erich Auerbach (1953/2003) *Mimesis: Representation of Reality in Western Literature* (trans.). New York: Doubleday: 495.

13 Bil Nichols (1991) *Representing Reality: Issues and Concepts in Documentary.* Bloomington: Indiana University Press: 4.

14 Williams, *Culture and Society*: 304.

15 Forsyth Hardy (1979) *John Grierson: A Documentary Biography.* London: Faber: 20.

16 Melanie Phillips (2006) The politics of bling. *Daily Mail*, May 22.

17 John Corner (2002) Performing the real: documentary diversions. *Television and New Media* 3(3): 257.

18 Ibid.

19 This was a documentary series which tracked a group of children into adulthood.

20 Lilie Chouliaraki (2006) Towards an analytics of mediation. *Critical Discourse Studies* 3(2): 153–178 at p. 000.

21 Ibid.: 178.

22 Ofcom (2009) *Ofcom's Second Public Broadcasting Review: Putting Viewers First.* London: HMSO: 21.

23 Sara Ahmed (1992) *The Cultural Politics of Emotion.* Edinburgh: Edinburgh University Press: 7.

24 Mohamed Elmasry (2002) *Anti-Islam in the Canadian MediaReport*: Montreal: Canadian Islamic Congress.

25 Mukti Jain Campion (2005) *Look Who's Talking: Cultural Diversity, Public Service Broadcasting and the National Conversation.* Project Report, Oxford: Nuffield College. Online at www.nuff.ox.ac.uk/Guardian/Campion/LookwhostalkingReport1/index1.html (accessed February 15, 2009).

26 Annabelle Sreberny (1999) *Include Me In.* London: Broadcasting Standards Council. Trevor McDonald is not only a highly experienced news presenter but is one of the longest-standing and best-known African Caribbean journalists in the UK.

27 Quoted in *Daily Telegraph*, March 5, 2007.

28 Bryan S. Turner (2002) Cosmopolitan virtue, globalization and patriotism. *Theory, Culture and Society* 19(1–2): 57.

29 Silverstone, *Media and Morality*: 59.

30 Marian Saward (1998) *The Terms of Democracy*. Cambridge: Polity Press: 61.

31 Ibid.: 21.

32 BBC, *Building Public Value*: 20.

33 John Hartley (2007) *Television Truths: Forms of Knowledge in Popular Culture*. Malden, MA: Blackwell: 52.

34 John Stuart Mill (1991) *On Liberty and Other Essays* (ed. J. Gray). Oxford: Oxford University Press: 328.

35 Mark Thompson (2008) The trouble with trust: building confidence in institutions. Speech given at QE2 Conference Centre, January 15.

36 Richard Sennett (1992) *The Fall of Public Man*. New York: W.W. Norton: 126.

37 Ibid.: 209.

38 Jacques Ranciere (2007) *Hatred of Democracy* (trans. Steve Corcoran). New York: W.W Norton & Co Inc.: 272.

39 John Durham Peters, (2001) Witnessing. *Media, Culture and Society* 23(6): 707–723.

40 Paul Levine (2008) A public voice for youth: the audience problem in digital media and civic education. In W.L. Bennett (ed.) *Civic Life Online: Learning How Digital Media Can Engage Youth*. Cambridge, MA: MIT Press: 119–138 at p. 130.

41 Howard Rheingold (2008) Using participatory media and public voice to encourage civic engagement. In W.L. Bennett (ed.) *Civic Life Online: Learning How Digital Media Can Engage Youth*. Cambridge, MA: MIT Press, 97–116.

42 Thompson, The trouble with trust.

43 Eric Donald Hirsch, Joseph F. Kett, and James S. Trefil (1988) *Cultural Literacy: What Every American Needs to Know*. New York: Vintage Books: 223.

44 Guy Debord (1983) *Society of the Spectacle*. London: Rebel Press: 40.

45 Peters, Witnessing: 708.

46 Saward, *The Terms of Democracy*: 21.

47 Cited in Deloitte Review and ITV Investigation (2007) *Use of Premium Rate Interactive Services in ITV Programming*. London: ITV: 60.

Bibliography

Ahmed, Sara (1992) *The Cultural Politics of Emotion*. Edinburgh: Edinburgh University Press.

Altheide, David (1995) *An Ecology of Communication: Cultural Formats of Control*, New York: Aldine.

Anderson, Benedict (1991) *Imagined Communities: Reflections on the Origin and Spread of Nationalism*. London: Verso.

Ang, Ien (1991) *Desperately Seeking the Audience*. London: Routledge.

Ang, Ien (1995) *Living Room Wars: Rethinking Media Audiences for a Postmodern World*. London: Routledge.

Arendt, Hannah (1958) *The Human Condition*. Chicago: Chicago University Press.

Armstrong, Cory L. (2004) The influence of reporter gender on source selection in newspaper stories. *Journalism and Mass Communication Quarterly* 81(1): 139–154.

Arnison, Matthew (2001) Open publishing is the same as free software. Online at www.cat.org.au/maffew/cat/openpub.html.

Asen, Robert (2000) Seeking the "counter" in counterpublics. *Communication Theory* 10(4): 425.

Atton, Chris (2002) *Alternative Media*. London: Sage.

Auerbach, Erich (1953/2003) *Mimesis: Representation of Reality in Western Literature* (trans.). New York: Doubleday.

Bagehot, Walter (1872) *The English Constitution*. http://bagehot.classicauthors.net/EnglishConstitution/EnglishConstitution1.html (accessed 29 September 2009).

Barlow, John Perry (1996) A Declaration of the Independence of Cyberspace. Online at http://homes.eff.org/~barlow/Declaration-Final.html (accessed August 20, 2008).

Barnett, Clive (2003) *Culture and Democracy: Media, Space and Representation*. Edinburgh: Edinburgh University Press.

170   *Bibliography*

Bauman, Zygmunt (2000) *Liquid Modernity*. Cambridge: Polity Press.

BBC (2004) *Building Public Value: Renewing the BBC for a Digital World*. London: BBC.

Benkler, Yochai (2006) *The Wealth of Networks: How Social Production Transforms Markets and Freedom*. New Haven, CT: Yale University Press.

Bennett, W. Lance (2003) New media power: the Internet and global activism. In Nick Couldry and James Curran (eds.) *Contesting Media Power: Alternative Media in a Networked World*. Lanham, MD: Rowman & Littlefield: 12–38.

Berger, Sarah (2005) From Aldermaston marcher to Internet activist. In Wilma de Jong, Martin Shaw, and Neil Stammers (eds.) *Global Activism, Global Media*. London, Ann Arbor, MI: Pluto Press, 84–91.

Bimber, Bruce Allen (1996) *Politics of Expertise in Congress: Rise and Fall of the Office of Technology Assessment*. Albany, NY: State University of New York Press.

Blumer, Herbert (1948) Public opinion and public opinion polling. *American Sociological Review*, 13(5): 542–549.

Blumler, Jay G. and Coleman, Stephen (2001) *Realising Democracy Online: A Civic Commons in Cyberspace*. London: Institute of Public Policy Research.

Boase, Jeffrey and Wellman, Barry (2006) Personal relationships: on and off the Internet. In Anita L. Vengelisti and Daniel Perlman (eds.) *The Cambridge Handbook of Personal Relationships*. Cambridge: Cambridge University Press: 709–726.

Bourdieu, P. (1971) Public opinion does not exist. In A. Matelart and S. Siegelaub (eds.) *Communication and Class Struggle*. New York: International General/IMMRC.

Bowman, Shane and Willis, Chris (2003) *We Media: How Audiences are Shaping the Future of News and Information*. Reston, VA: The Media Center at the American Press Institute.

Brecht, Bertolt (1932) Der Rundfunk als Kommunikationsapparat, *Bjitter des Hessischen Landestheaters Darmstadt*, 16, July.

Brecht, Bertolt, (1936) Radiotheorie 1927–1932. *Gesammelte Werke Band*, 1: 117–124.

Briggs, Asa (1961) *The Birth of Broadcasting*. Oxford: Oxford University Press.

Briggs, Asa (1985) *The BBC: A Short Story of the First Fifty Years*. Oxford: Oxford University Press.

Browne, Donald R. (2005) *Ethnic Minorities, Electronic Media and the Public Sphere: A Comparative Approach*. Cresskill, NJ: Hampton Press.

Bruns, Axel (2005) *Gatewatching: Collaborative Online News Production*. Oxford: Peter Lang.

Bruns, Axel (2007) Methodologies for mapping the political blogosphere. *First Monday*, 12(5). Online at http://firstmonday.org/issues/issue12_5/bruns/index.html (accessed August 20, 2008).

Buckingham-Shum, Simon (2007) Hypermedia discourse: contesting networks of ideas and arguments. In Uta Priss, Simon Polovina, and Richard Hill (eds.) *Conceptual Structures: Knowlede Architectures for Smart Applications. Proceedings of the 15th International Conference on Conceptual Structures.* Berlin: Springer-Verlag: 29–44. Online at www.springerlink.com/content/ x16xr44xp680/?p=165e5f2693254571992406f8a01af936&pi=0 (accessed September 10, 2008).

Bucy, Erik and Gregson, Kimberly (2001) Media participation: a legitimizing mechanism of mass democracy. *New Media and Society* 3(2): 357–380.

Burgess, Jean (2006) Hearing ordinary voices. *Continuum* 20(2): 201–214.

Calhoun, Craig (2007) Community without propinquity revisited: communications technology and the transformation of the urban public sphere. *Sociological Inquiry*, 68(3): 374–397.

Campion, Mukti Jain (2005) *Look Who's Talking: Cultural Diversity, Public Service Broadcasting and the National Conversation.* Project Report, Oxford: Nuffield College. Online at www.nuff.ox.ac.uk/Guardian/Campion/ LookwhostalkingReport1/index1.html (accessed February 15, 2009).

Carlyle, Thomas (1897) *Latter-day Pamphlets. Chartism.* Boston: deWolfe, Fiske.

Carpignano, Paulo, Anderson, Robin, Aronowitz, Stanley, and DeFazio, William (1990) Chatter in the age of electronic reproduction: talk television and the public mind. In Bruce Robins (ed.) *The Phantom Public Sphere.* Minneapolis: University of Minnesota Press: 93–120.

Carvin, Andy. How the Internet is changing the playing field. Online at www. america.gov/st/usg-english/2008/April/20080523104429WRybakcuH0. 324383.html (accessed September 21, 2009).

Castells, Manuel (2000) *The Rise of the Network Society: The Information Age: Economy, Society and Culture,* vol. 1. Malden, MA: Wiley-Blackwell.

Chadwick, Andrew (2006) *Internet Politics: States, Citizens and New Communication Technologies.* New York and Oxford: Oxford University Press.

Chouliaraki, Lilie (2006) Towards an analytics of mediation. *Critical Discourse Studies* 3(2): 153–178.

Coleman, Stephen (2004) Connecting Parliament to the public via the Internet. *Information, Communication and Society* 7(1): 1–22.

Coleman, Stephen and Blumler, Jay G. (2008) *The Internet and Democratic Citizenship: Theory, Practice and Policy.* Cambridge: Cambridge University Press.

Coleman, Stephen and Moss, Giles (2008) Governing at a distance: politicians in the blogosphere. *Information Polity* 13(1–2): 7–20.

Corner, John (2002) Performing the real: documentary diversions. *Television and New Media* 3(3): 255–270.

Dahlgren, Peter (2005) The Internet, public spheres, and political communication: dispersion and deliberation, *Political Communication* 22(2): 147–162.

Daniels, George L. (2006) The role of Native American print and online media in the "era of big stories": a comparative case study of Native American outlets' coverage of the Red Lake shootings. *Journalism* 7(3): 321–342.

Dayan, Daniel (2005) Mothers, midwives and abortionists: genealogy, obstetrics, audiences and publics. In Sonia Livingstone (ed.) *Audiences and Publics: When Cultural Engagement Matters for the Public Sphere*. Bristol: Intellect: 41–75.

De Jong, Wilma, Shaw, Martin and Stammers, Neil (eds.) (2005) *Global Activism, Global Media*. London, Ann Arbor, MI: Pluto Press.

Debord, Guy (1983) *Society of the Spectacle* (trans.). London: Rebel Press.

Deloitte Review and ITV Investigation (2007) *Use of Premium Rate Interactive Services in ITV Programming*. London: ITV.

Dewey, John (1927) *The Public and Its Problems*. London: H. Holt & Co.

Downing, John (2001) *Radical Media: Rebellious Communication and Social Movements*. London and New York: Sage.

Drezner, Daniel W. and Farrell, Henry (2008) Introduction: Blogs, politics and power. *Public Choice* 134: 1–13.

Duncombe, Stephen (1996) *Notes from Underground: Zines and the Politics of Alternative Culture*. London: Verso.

Ellis, John (2000) *Seeing Things: Television in the Age of Uncertainty*. London: I.B. Tauris.

Elmasry, Mohamed (2002) *Anti-Islam in the Candian MediaReport*: Montreal: Canadian Islamic Congress.

Enzensberger, Hans Magnus, (1970) Constituents of a theory of the media. *New Left Review* 1(64).

Etzioni, Amitai (1972) MINERVA: an electronic town hall. *Policy Sciences* 3(4): 18.

Feldman, Sally (2000) Twin peaks: The staying power of BBC Radio 4's *Woman's Hour*. In Caroline Mitchell (ed.) *Women and Radio: Airing Differences*. London and New York: Routledge: 64–72.

Felski, Rita (1989) *Beyond Feminist Aesthetic: Feminist Literature and Social Change*. London: Radius.

Fiske, John (1987) *Television Culture*. London and New York: Routledge.

Forde, Susan (1998) The development of the alternative press in Australia. *Media International Australia* 87: 114–33.

Forde, Susan, Foxwell, Kerrie and Meadows, Michael (2003) Through the lens of the local: public arena journalism in the Australian community broadcasting sector. *Journalism* 4(3): 314–335.

Foucault, M. (2002) *Archaeology of Knowledge*. New York and London: Routledge.

Fyfe, Nicholas and Bannister, Jon (1996) City watching: CCTV surveillance in public spaces. *Area* 28(1): 37–46.

Gaber, Ivor and Wynne Willson, A. (2005) Dying for diamonds: the mainstream media and NGOs – A case study of Action Aid. In Wilma de Jong, Martin Shaw, and Neil Stammers (eds.) *Global Activism, Global Media*. London, Ann Arbor, MI: Pluto Press: 95–109.

Gibbs, Patricia L. (2003) Alternative things considered: a political economic analysis of labour processes and relations at a Honolulu alternative newspaper. *Media, Culture and Society* 25(5): 587–605.

Giddens, A. (1990) *The Consequences of Modernity*. Cambridge: Polity Press.

Giddens, A. (1991) *Modernity and Self-Identity*. Cambridge: Polity Press.

Gillmore, Dan (2004) *We the Media: Grassroots Journalism by the People, for the People*. Sebastopol, CA: O'Reilly.

Ginsberg, Benjamin (1998) *The Captive Public: How Mass Opinion Promotes State Power*. New York: Basic Books.

Girard, Bruce (ed.) (1992) *A Passion for Radio: Radio Waves and Community*. Montreal: Black Rose Books.

Glasgow University Media Group (1976) *Bad News*. London: Routledge & Kegan Paul.

Glasgow University Media Group (1982) *Really Bad News*. London: Routledge & Kegan Paul.

Glasgow University Media Group (1985) *War and Peace News*. Milton Keynes: Open University Press.

Goffman, Erving (1981) *Forms of Talk*. Oxford: Blackwell.

Graham, Andrew (2000) *The Future of Communications: Public Service Broadcasting*. Luton: University of Luton Press.

Groombridge, Brian (1972) *Television and the People*. London: Penguin.

Gurevitch, Michael (1982) *Culture, Society, and the Media*. London and New York: Routledge.

Habermas, Jürgen (1991) *The Structural Transformation of the Public Sphere: An Inquiry Into a Category of Bourgeois Society*. Cambridge, MA: MIT Press.

Habermas, Jürgen (1996) *Between Facts and Norms: Contributions to a Discourse Theory of Law and Democracy* (trans.). Cambridge, MA: MIT Press.

Halperin, John (1982) *Gissing: A Life in Books*. Oxford: Oxford University Press.

Hardy, Forsyth (1979) *John Grierson: A Documentary Biography*. London: Faber.

Hartley, John (2007) *Television Truths: Forms of Knowledge in Popular Culture*. Malden, MA: Blackwell.

Herbst, Susan (1993) *Numbered Voices: How Opinion Polling Has Shaped American Politics*. Chicago: University of Chicago Press.

Hirsch, Eric Donald, Kett, Joseph F., and Trefil, James S. (1988) *Cultural Literacy: What Every American Needs to Know*. New York: Vintage Books.

Horton, Donald and Wohl, Richard R. (1956) Mass communication and parasocial interaction: observations on intimacy at a distance. *Psychiatry* 19(3): 215–229.

Howley, Kevin (2003) A poverty of voices: street newspapers as communicative democracy. *Journalism* 4(3): 273–292.

Hutchins, Brett and Lester, Libby (2006) Environmental protest and tap-dancing with the media in the information age. *Media, Culture and Society* 28(3): 433–451.

Jallov, Birgitte (1992) Community radio as a tool for feminist messages. In Nick Jankowski, Ole Prehn, and James Stappers (eds.) *The People's Voice: Local Radio and Television in Europe.* Luton: John Libbey & Co., 215–224.

Jankowski, N. (2002) The conceptual contours of community radio. In Nicholas Jankowski with Ole Prehn (2002) *Community Media in the Information Age: Perspectives and Prospects.* Cresskill, NJ: Hampton Press, 3–16.

Jankowski, N., Prehn, Ole, and Stappers, James (eds.) (1992) *The People's Voice: Local Radio and Television in Europe.* Luton: John Libbey & Co.

Jephson, Henry (1892) *The Platform: Its Rise and Progress,* vol. 1. London: Macmillan.

Johnson, Thomas J. and Kaye, Barbara (2003) Around the World Wide Web in 80 ways: How motives for going online are linked to Internet activities among politically interested Internet users. *Social Science Computer Review* 21(3): 304–325.

Kant, I. (1781/2007) *Critique of Pure Reason.* London: Penguin.

Kavanaugh, Andrea L. and Patterson, Scott J. (2001) The impact of community computer networks on social capital and community involvement. *American Behavioral Scientist* (45)3: 496–509.

Kohn, Margaret (2003) *Radical Space.* Ithaca, NY: Cornell University Press.

Kraut, Robert, Steinfield, Charles, Chan, Alice, Butlery, Brian, and Hoag, Ann (1998) Coordination and virtualization: the role of electronic networks and personal relationships. *Journal of Computer-Mediated Communication* 3(4). Online at www3.interscience.wiley.com/cgi-bin/fulltext/120837744/ HTMLSTART (accessed September 15, 2008).

Krieger, Bernhard and Muller, Phillip S. (2003) Making internet communities work: reflections on an unusual business model. *ACM SIGMIS Database* 34(2): 50–59.

Kung-Shackleman, Lucy (2000) *Inside the BBC and CNN.* London and New York: Routledge.

La Vopa, Anthony J. (1992) Conceiving a public: ideas and society in eighteenth-century Europe. *Journal of Modern History* 64(10): 79–116.

Le Bon, Gustave (1895, 1991) *Psychologie des foules.* Paris: PUF.

Lefort, Claude (1986) *The Political Forms of Modern Society.* Cambridge, MA: MIT Press.

Levine, Paul (2008) A public voice for youth: the audience problem in digital media and civic education. In W. Lance Bennett (ed.) *Civic Life Online: Learning How Digital Media Can Engage Youth.* Cambridge, MA: MIT Press: 119–138.

Livingstone, Sonia (ed.) (2005). *Audiences and Publics: When Cultural Engagement Matters for the Public Sphere*. Bristol: Intellect.

Livingstone, Sonia and Lunt, Peter (1994) *Talk on Television*. London: Routledge.

Livingstone, Sonia, (ed.) (2005) *Audiences and Publics: Changing Media*, vol. 2. London: Intellect.

McCauley, Michael, P., Peterson, Eric E., Artz, B. Lee, and Halleck, DeeDee (eds.) (2003) *Public Broadcasting and the Public Interest*. New York and London: M.E. Sharpe.

McClelland, John S. (1998) *A History of Western Political Thought*. London and New York: Routledge.

MacKuen, Michael B. (1990) Speaking of politics: individual conversational choice, public opinion, and the prospects for deliberative democracy. In John A. Ferejohn and James H. Kuklinski (eds.) *Information and Democratic Processes*. Urbana, IL: University of Illinois Press: 59–99.

Manin, Bernard (1997) *The Principles of Representative Government*. Cambridge: Cambridge University Press.

Mill, John Stuart (1991) *On Liberty and Other Essays* (ed. J. Gray). Oxford: Oxford University Press.

Millward, Peter (2008) The rebirth of the football fanzine: using e-zines as data source. *Journal of Sport and Social Issues* 32(3): 299–310.

Mitchell, Caroline (2000) *Women and Radio: Airing Differences*. London and New York: Routledge.

Mitchell, Don (1995) The end of public space? People's Park, definitions of the public and democracy. *Annals of the Association of American Geographers* 85(1): 108–133.

Morrison, David, Kieran, Matthew, Svennevig, Michael and Ventress, Sarah (2007) *Media and Values: Intimate Transgressions in a Changing Moral and Cultural Landscape*. London: Intellect.

Murdock, Graham (1999) Rights and representations: public discourse and cultural citizenship. In Jostein Gripsrud (ed.) *Television and Common Knowledge*. London: Routledge: 7–17.

Negt, Oskar and Kluge, Alexander (1993) *Public Sphere and Experience: Toward an Analysis of the Bourgeois and Proletarian Public Sphere*. Minneapolis, MN: University of Minnesota Press.

Nichols, Bil (1991) *Representing Reality: Issues and Concepts in Documentary*. Bloomington, IN: Indiana University Press.

Nie, Norman, and Erbring, Lutz (2000, March). Internet and society: A preliminary report Online at www.stanford.edu/group/siqss/Press_Release/Preliminary_Report.pdf (accessed July 28, 2008).

Ofcom (2009) *Ofcom's Second Public Broadcasting Review: Putting Viewers First*. London: HMSO.

Ojo, Tokunbo (2006) Ethnic print media in the multicultural nation of Canada: a case study of the black newspaper in Montreal. *Journalism* 7(3): 343–361.

Orlikowski. Wanda (1992) Learning from Notes: organizational issues in groupware implementation. Computer-supported cooperative work. *Proceedings of the 1992 ACM Conference on Computer-Supported Work*. Ontario: Association of Computer Machinery.

Ouellette, Laurie (2002) *Viewers Like You? How Public TV Failed the People*. New York: Columbia University Press.

Ozouf, Mona (1989) *L'homme régénéré: Essais sur la révolution française*. Paris: Gallimard.

Peters, John Durham (2001) Witnessing. *Media, Culture and Society* 23(6): 707–723.

Phillips, Melanie (2006) The politics of bling. *Daily Mail*, May 22.

Pickering, Michael and Chaney, David (1986) Democracy and communication: Mass Observation. *Journal of Communication* 36(1): 42.

Pickles, Wilfred (1950) *Between You and Me*. London: Werner Laurie.

Plotz, John (2000) *The Crowd: British Literature and Public Politics*. Berkeley, CA: University of California Press.

Postman, Neil (1985) *Amusing Ourselves to Death*, New York: Viking.

Power, Mary, Power, Des, and Horstmanshof, Louise (2007) Deaf people communicating via SMS, TTY, relay service, fax and computers in Australia. *Journal of Deaf Studies and Deaf Education* 12(1): 80–92.

Quan-Haase, Anabel and Wellman, Barry (2004) How does the Internet affect social capital? In Marleen Hysman and Volker Wulf (eds.) *Social Capital and Information Technology*. Cambridge, MA: MIT Press: 113–132.

Ranciere, Jacques (2007) *Hatred of Democracy* (trans. Steve Corcoran). New York: W.W. Norton & Co Inc.

Reith, John C.W. (1949) *Into the Wind: Memoirs*. London: Hodder & Stoughton.

Rheingold, Howard (2008) Using participatory media and public voice to encourage civic engagement. In W.L. Bennett (ed.) *Civic Life Online: Learning How Digital Media Can Engage Youth*. Cambridge, MA: MIT Press, 97–116.

Richardson, J.E. (2001) "Now is the time to put an end to all this": argumentative discourse theory and "letters to the editor." *Discourse and Society* 12(2): 143–168.

Rorty, Richard (1989) *Contingency, Irony, and Solidarity*. Cambridge: Cambridge University Press.

Rose, Nikolas (1999) *The Powers of Freedom*. Cambridge: Cambridge University Press.

Ross, Karen (2007) The journalist, the housewife, the citizen and the press: women and men as sources in local news narratives. *Journalism* 8(4): 449–514.

Royal Commission on the Press (1977). London: HMSO.

Ruiz, Pollyanna (2005) Bridging the gap: from the margins to the mainstream. In Wilma de Jong, Martin Shaw, and Neil Stammers (eds.) *Global Activism, Global Media.* London, Ann Arbor, MI: Pluto Press: 194–207.

Sack, Warren (2000) Conversation Map: an interface for very large-scale conversations. *Journal of Management Information Systems* 17(3): 73–92.

Saward, Marian (1998) *The Terms of Democracy.* Cambridge: Polity Press.

Scannell, Paddy (1996) *Radio, Television, and Modern Life: A Phenomenological Approach.* Oxford: Blackwell.

Scannell, Paddy (2000) For-anyone-as-someone structures. *Media, Culture and Society,* 23(1): 95–24.

Scannell, Paddy (2004) *Big Brother* as a television event. *New Media and Society* 3(3): 271–282.

Scannell, Paddy and Cardiff, David (1991) *A Social History of British Broadcasting,* vol. 1: *1922–39: Serving the Nation.* Oxford: Blackwell.

Schilt, Kristen (2003) "I'll resist with every inch and every breath." Girls and zine-making as a form of resistance. *Youth and Society* 35(1): 71–97.

Sennett, Richard (1992) *The Fall of Public Man.* New York: W.W. Norton.

Shah, Dhavan V., Kwak, Nojin, and Holbert, R. Lance (2001) "Connecting" and "disconnecting" with civic life: patterns of Internet use and the production of social capital. *Political Communication* 18(2): 141–162.

Shahin, Jamal and Neuhold, Christine (2007) Connecting Europe: the use of "new" information and communication technologies within European Parliament Standing Committees. *Journal of Legislative* Studies 13(3): 388–402.

Shirky, Clay (2005) Ontology is overrated: categories, links and tags. Online at www.shirky.com/writings/ontology_overrated.htm (accessed August 20, 2008).

Shklovski, Irina, Kraut, Robert, and Rainie, Lee (2004) The Internet and social participation: contrasting cross-sectional and longitudinal analyses. *Journal of Computer Mediated Communication* 10(1). Online at http://jcmc.indiana.edu/vol10/issue1/shklovski_kraut.html (accessed September 9, 2008).

Silverstone, Roger (2007) *Media and Morality: On the Rise of the Mediapolis.* Cambridge: Polity Press.

Sreberny, Annabelle (1999) *Include Me In.* London: Broadcasting Standards Council.

Summerfield, Penny (1985) Mass Observation: social research or social movement? *Journal of Contemporary History* 20(3): 448.

Sunstein, Cass (2001) Democracy and the Internet. *Mots Pluriel* 18, August. Online at www.arts.uwa.edu.au/MotsPluriels/MP1801cs.html (accessed August 20, 2008).

Swithinbank, Tessa (1996) World exclusive. *New Internationalist.* February: 28–30.

Taine, Hippolyte (1881/1972) *The Ancient Regime* (trans. John Durand). Freeport, NY: Books for Libraries Press.

Thompson, John B. (1995) *The Media and Modernity: A Social Theory of the Media.* Cambridge: Polity Press.

Thompson, John B. (2005) The new visibility. *Theory, Culture and Society* 22(1): 31–51.

Thompson, Mark (2008) The trouble with trust: building confidence in institutions. Speech given at QE2 Conference Centre, January 15.

Tilly, Charles (1983) Speaking your mind without elections, surveys or social movements. *Public Opinion Quarterly* 47(4): 474.

Turner, Bryan S. (2002) Cosmopolitan virtue, globalization and patriotism. *Theory, Culture and Society* 19(1–2): 45–63.

UNESCO (1980) *Many Voices One World: Towards a New, More Just and More Efficient World Information and Communication Order* (the MacBride Commission). Lanham, MD: Rowman & Littlefield.

Verba, Sidney (1996) The citizen as respondent: sample surveys and American democracy: presidential address to the American Political Science Association, 1995. *American Political Science Review* 90(1): 1.

Wahl-Jorgensen, Karin (2002) The construction of the public in letters to the editor: deliberative democracy and the idiom of insanity. *Journalism* 3(2): 183–204.

Waltz, Mitzi (2005) *Alternative and Activist Media.* Edinburgh: Edinburgh University Press.

Warner, Michael (2002) *Publics and Counterpublics.* Cambridge, MA: MIT Press.

Wellman, Barry, Boase, Jeffrey, and Chen, Wenhans (2002) The networked nature of community online and offline. *IT and Society* 1(1): 1–15.

Williams, Raymond (1961) *Culture and Society, 1780–1950.* London: Penguin Books.

Wood, Helen (2007) The mediated conversational floor: an interactive approach to audience reception analysis. *Media, Culture and Society* 29(1): 75–103.

Index